If
Morning
Never
Comes

If Morning Never Comes

A Near-Death Experience in Vietnam

By Bill VandenBush

THE OLD HUNDRED AND ONE PRESS

North Platte, Nebraska

Published by the Old 101 Press
13680 North Sandhill Drive
North Platte, NE 69101

Printed in the United State of America

Cover Design by Diane Solomon
Book Design by Kai Crozer
Edited by Norman D. Farley PhD

Library of Congress Control Number: 2003109753
Bill VandenBush
If Morning Never Comes / by Bill VandenBush
p. cm
Summary: A soldier's story of his near-death experience in Vietnam and the insights and lessons learned from his excursion into a dimension of enlightenment.

ISBN 0-9721613-4-1

This book is dedicated to
Donna VandenBush, my mom,
who always loved me unconditionally

I wish to acknowledge the following people for their contributions to the completion of this book:

Lynne Martins, for getting me started. Norm Farley, for your editorial help and undying friendship. David Gronseth, who found the mistakes the rest of us missed. Ken Peterson, for believing in me. Shannon Anderson, for never having doubts. Jeff Montgomery, for your connections and great sense of timing. Norm Wear and Myrna Glassburg, for making me part of your family. Diane Solomon, for your incredible artwork. Dariela Rodriguez, for listening to all my ideas. Billie Thornburg and Ann Milton, for supporting this project. Nora Anderson, for your endearing friendship. Dr. Mark Brooks, for keeping me healthy. All my dear friends who have encouraged and guided me through this enormous undertaking.

Introduction

On April 17, 1969, my life was forever changed by a devastating war injury and the subsequent near-death experience that connected me with the Light of the spiritual dimension. This story chronicles the events that led to my enlistment in the U.S. Army at a time when being a soldier was an unpopular career choice, and the incredible journey that helped me to understand the meaning of life.

It is my sincere hope that you will find this book entertaining, spiritually enlightening, inspirational, and full of guiding wisdom. I tell my story and share my experiences so that you may be guided to find your own higher purpose in life. I believe that my war injuries and the long process of healing, both physically and spiritually, were not an accident. Although they didn't seem like it at the time, my war injuries and the horrors I experienced in the Vietnam War were a wonderful gift given to me from the spiritual dimension. That gift has not only enhanced my life, but the lives of most of the people I have spent time with over the years.

In writing this book, I have tried to give you a clear understanding of the nature of the human Spirit, and the nature of being human in spite of that Spirit. It shows how we each have our own unique way of dealing with spiritual issues. I don't relate Spirit to religion because I believe that the core of all religions have a spiritual aspect, thus, the Spirit I refer to is a universal being and is not bound by any religious constraint.

The Spirit has taught me that all human beings share a common spiritual connection, although for some it is much stronger than for others. The strength of our spiritual connectedness can be enhanced by simply being aware of the spiritual messages being sent by the people with whom we come in contact.

It took me twenty years to finally tell this story to another human being. It took another ten years of urging from the people who heard this story to get me to write this book. The words and stories in this book are my way to share my gift with you. Please enjoy this book and accept the special gift it has to give.

John Lear, Hank Lousko, and Bill VandenBush
Soldiers for a moment, friends for eternity.

AMBUSH
By Bill VandenBush

Babes crying break the still of the warm night air

The smell of death hangs heavy while soldiers wait

Anxiety is shrouded by a black moonless sky

Cold blue steel clutched tightly prepared to light the darkness

Fear makes hearts pound loudly

An eternity will pass before the sun rises

A soldier holds many thoughts in the night
he dreams of the love he left behind,
not just the love of a woman
but the love of country, of home.

He dreams of the sweet smell of new mown grass
on a warm summer day, of picnics in the park
and strolling hand in hand with the girl he loves.

He dreams of home cooked meals and holidays
with family and friends, of a warm fire
on a cool winter night in the safety of his own home.

The night of war is cruel.

For some it passes with the coming of daylight.
but for most, it haunts the corners of the mind,
manifesting itself in times of stress,creating havoc in the soul.

Babes crying break the still of the warm night air

AMBUSH!!

Chapter 1

Saying Good-bye

I checked my duffle bag at the airline counter and headed to the passenger terminal. As I walked through Orange County Airport in Southern California, I smelled the subtle aroma of freshly popped popcorn smothered with sweet butter. The airport terminal was filled with bright sunlight beaming in through the tall windows facing the runway. The sound of my leather-soled shoes slapping against the hard floor reminded me of how I had learned to march in perfect cadence.

My mom, three brothers and my sister had accompanied me to the airport and followed me to the passenger terminal. In twenty minutes they would be waving good-bye as I boarded a northbound commuter plane on my way to Oakland to join the rest of the troops headed for Vietnam. Ironically, this airport was later named John Wayne Airport after the man who influenced me to become a soldier and go fight in the Vietnam War.

My summer khakis fit me well and although soldiers were not held in high esteem in the summer of 1968, I was proud to be serving my country and wearing the uniform of the United States Army.

I was only eighteen, but Army training had aged me, given me an adult presence and a tough edge. I felt relaxed and confident as the late July sun warmed the waiting area of the terminal. I reassured my mother that I was going to return home in a year just as healthy and strong as I was on this glorious day.

Mom was very distraught at the thought of her first-born son going to a foreign land to fight a senseless war. We had already lost many good young men. She was worried sick I would join the rolls of the dead recited daily on the evening news.

Shelly and Jan, two high school girlfriends, and my buddy Larry joined my family at the passenger terminal to see me off. I knew Shelly had a crush on me. She had made her intentions known the previous night, but I didn't want any serious involvements distracting me from my duties as a combat infantry soldier. I was playing it cool.

The overhead speakers announced that my flight to Oakland was ready to board and it dawned on me, "This might be the last time I ever see my family or any of my friends."

It was only a fleeting thought and I immediately brushed it from my mind. I couldn't afford to think about the "what if's." I had to keep my mind on the task at hand; get to Oakland and the Army would tell me exactly what to do from then on.

I gave Mom and the girls a quick hug, shook hands with Larry and headed for the gate, waving goodbye to my siblings as I went.

Boarding the plane I didn't look back. I knew my mom and the girls would be crying. I was scared but I didn't want anyone to know how I felt. I wanted to be remembered as a brave soldier.

The airplane was a small turbo-prop that held about twenty passengers and made several stops between Orange County and Oakland. The flight was two and a half hours long and I didn't really want to talk to anyone. There were only fifteen passengers on this leg of the flight so I was able to find a seat in the back where I could sit by myself and think without interruption.

I took the window seat and left the aisle seat open, hoping no one would sit there. At this particular time in history no one went out of his or her way to sit next to a soldier anyway.

It had only been a little over a year since I graduated from high school. I started thinking about graduation day and all the events that had brought me to this point in such a short time. As the plane lifted off, graduation day seemed like a distant memory from another time or another life but the memory was clear and I found myself drifting back to high school commencement.

Summer 1967

The commencement ceremony was almost over. I didn't care one bit whether I had a diploma or not. All I could think about was getting out to my car and driving north to pick up my long time friend, Bob. We were headed for the Monterey Pop Festival where we had great tickets near the stage for every concert. Three days of rock-and-roll and no parents to tell us what to do or how to behave. This was ecstasy! This weekend would make 1967 one of the best years of my life.

The trip was a great teenage adventure. Bob and I had been close childhood friends but had been separated just before our freshman year in high school when my family moved thirty miles south from El Monte to Santa Ana. The Monterey journey was the first time we were actually going someplace together on our own. We were both quite excited about spending three days, unchaperoned, in Monterey.

The drive up the coast took eight hours. Bob and I had a wonderful time talking and feeling free from the chains of school and parents. We ate junk food and drank Cokes all the way.

It was odd, I thought, that my ideals were so innocent. All I wanted to do was listen to the music and have a good time.

I wanted to soak in the hippie culture and hear the professors of peace and free love.

Only a few miles from the arena where the pop festival was being held was Fort Ord, one of the Army's major training posts. At the time, my thoughts couldn't have been farther away from anything military, but in nine short months I would be entering the front gates of Fort Ord as a member of the United States Army.

The Monterey Pop Festival was even better than I had imagined. The music and light shows were spectacular, but what was most amazing to me was the never-ending string of booze and drugs being passed up and down the aisles. It all seemed perfectly natural at the time. This was clearly the most exciting thing Bob and I had ever done and the Pop Festival experience set the tone for the rest of the summer.

I was a hippie, a '60s teen, a child of love and a free spirit. I grew my hair long, wore bell-bottom pants, paisley shirts and headbands and played the tambourine. I listened to rock and roll, Folk and psychedelic music. My friends and I went to the hills where we had sing-a-longs and love-ins.

The psychedelic and folk music of the '60s was very important to me. It allowed me to go to places in my mind that I couldn't go in my body. With music I could be a dreamer, getting lost in the music and dreaming of an idealistic life.

The music of the '60s catered to the dreamer and idealist; I was guilty of being both. I also believed that if I worked hard and made a good living, I would be prosperous and get all the things I wanted from life.

I wanted to accomplish something in life. I wanted to be respected, but had no real desire for fame and fortune. Believe it or not, at the age of eighteen, my ultimate desire was to be a middle-class American, to have a house, a car, a wife and children. I was a hippie and an innocent young man.

The summer of 1967 was a wild time. With high school behind me I wanted to know what the world had to offer. There wasn't an inkling of thought given to going to college. I wasn't a good student and although I graduated from high school, I was closer to the bottom of my class than the top.

I enjoyed the lazy summer days hanging around with friends but I also wanted money to spend on my car, dates and other activities. Dad spent most of our family's disposable income on beer so there wasn't much left for allowances.

I had always held some kind of job while in high school and the prospect of getting work and making money was appealing to me. I tried factory work, but that was boring.

I looked around at several options and finally took a job at a large dry cleaning company as a driver's assistant. The job was easy, the pay was better than average and they didn't seem to mind my long hair and casual dress. I was a good worker and was soon promoted to managing my own small department, household goods. I enjoyed going to the customers' homes to pick up draperies, bedspreads and other goods to be cleaned and I became very proficient at pressing draperies.

The work was enjoyable and I was well liked in the company, but I couldn't quite get comfortable with making a career in the dry cleaning business. I worked there about three months and kept getting a sense that there was something else I was supposed to be doing. There was something still unsettled within me, something quietly pushing me to make a change.

One evening after work I took a drive down the coast by myself to think. This was something I had done often when I needed time to think about my life.

As I was passing through San Juan Capistrano, I heard a gentle voice that seemed to come from inside my head; it said, "Follow your Spirit."

I was surprised and wasn't quite sure what was happening. I suddenly felt a deep calm and was awash in an air of warmth.

This was a new experience for me and I felt something stirring deep within. It wasn't a conscious thing but more like a subtle nudge. It was probably the first time I had a sense that there was something connected to me that was beyond life on this earth. I wondered if this was what people meant when they talked about a "spiritual awakening."

Since I was never a very religious sort it was hard for me to put a religious or God connection to this message from within. Religion always seemed so contrived to me. I felt that if this all loving, all mighty God they talked about in church was all they said He was, He would be glad to talk to me and hear from me everyday, not just on Sunday when I put on a suit and went to *His* house.

I didn't think much more about this voice but kept what it said in the back of my mind. I may not have been very religious but I was a very spiritual person in my own way. Little did I know I was following my destiny.

I returned to work the next day with a renewed sense of purpose and a deeper awareness of my daily life. I worked with a greater sense of commitment but was acutely aware that, in time, the Spirit would present new options.

Protests

In late autumn of '67 the Vietnam War was escalating and the group I hung out with began to protest the war. We were not a part of the vocal minority that took over college campuses and spit on returning veterans. Mostly, our protests consisted of riding up into the hills on weekends or after work where we would join other groups, sing protest songs and smoke marijuana. In our own naive way, we thought we were making a difference.

As I spent time with my hippie friends and continued to protest the Vietnam War, I began to ask myself questions, "What is the war all about?" and, "Where in hell is Vietnam?"

I'd never even heard of the country of Vietnam before the war gained public awareness. I knew it was in Southeast Asia but didn't have much of a reference because I was not well traveled. My only knowledge of what existed beyond the boundaries of the Western United States was what I had seen on television.

Protesting the war was more social than political for me; it was an opportunity to spend time with friends, meet new people and discuss the ideals we thought were best for the people of the world. I didn't *really* know what it meant to protest this war and why this war wasn't right. I had heard all the other wars were right: World War I was right, World War II was right, Korea was right, so how come Vietnam wasn't right?

The John Wayne Generation

I grew up in the John Wayne generation, learning about war from the Hollywood perspective where every man was a hero and every soldier was adored by his nation and its people. I was greatly influenced by John Wayne's macho image.

I hadn't had any positive male influences or mentors in my life to direct or shape me. Since Dad was an alcoholic and not a good role model, this Hollywood hero was all I had to look up to.

Patriotism was strongly ingrained in me by the war movies which was probably why I questioned the protests. I believed fighting wars was the *right* thing to do and defending my country was my duty as an American.

Even though I protested the war, I held firm that joining the military was respectable and what honorable men did. I believed serving in the armed forces was a rite of passage to become a real man. I believed military service was how boys like me became men and gained the respect I so desperately desired.

This Hollywood influence and unrealistic perspective of war coupled with the reality of the Vietnam protests was confusing. Who was right, the movie heroes or the protestors?

Sure, I watched the TV coverage of the war on the evening news just like everyone else. I saw soldiers marching, running, getting shot and carrying their wounded off the battleground, all in glorious black and white, but it had little impact on me.

I had no concept of what real war was about. All my ideas about war had come from television and the imagination of Hollywood. My virgin ideas about the purpose of war were idealistic and naive.

I understood nothing about the human component of war or the brutality that the Vietnam War or any war could inflict on a young man. Vietnam didn't seem real at all. It was just a picture on a television screen, just like a John Wayne movie.

The Spirit Moves

One day in early 1968, I had an argument with my father, a real blowout. This was the final straw. I knew I would have to leave home for good this time.

My father and I hadn't gotten along well for several years. He didn't like my long hair, my bell-bottom pants and what *he* thought were my anti-establishment ideals. He wanted me to be an upstanding citizen by conforming to the norms of his generation's society. Of course, I didn't even know what those norms were, other than having a short haircut, wearing a dress shirt and tie and being respectful of my elders.

For many years I had resisted the control that my father sought to impose on my life. All I wanted was to be my own person, independent of his control and away from his constant reminders of how much I owed him for raising me. In short, I was fed up with his overwhelming criticism of my friends, my lifestyle and me.

I was also tiring of the "Vietnam Protest." I really did *not* understand what the war was all about. I was frustrated and I questioned our country's involvement in Vietnam.

I felt like my protests weren't valid because I was unable to fully comprehend *why* our country chose to expend so many human lives and financial resources in such a tiny, out-of-the-way country. There didn't seem to be any clear-cut goals in this war and the country was not behind it as it was for other wars.

I began to think the only way to understand *this* war was to obtain firsthand experience. I thought if I did this, my protests would seem more valid and more credible. I also believed this would allow me to make the break from my family and become my own man. Just like John Wayne, I could join the cause and fight for God and country.

After the big argument with my father, I went to talk with my buddy, Dennis, (who was also angry with his father) and after a brief discussion, we decided we didn't want to have anything to do with our fathers. We decided to quit our jobs and sign up for military service.

I never discussed my plan to join the military and go to war with an adult nor did I ask an adult for an opinion or advice. I believed that I had no one to ask and also that I did not *need* to ask permission from adults. After all, I was eighteen (just barely) and had a right to make my own decisions about how I spent my life.

It was then that I felt the Spirit move again, "Follow your Spirit," quietly whispering in the depths of my soul.

The Buddy Plan

Dennis and I started out with the Air Force recruiter. We took the tests and filled out all the forms. In about a week, the recruiter told us we'd scored high marks on the tests and that we were fine candidates for the Air Force but we'd have about a six month wait before we could get in.

That was too long for us, so we went to the Navy recruiter. We took the tests, scored well, received an invitation to join but, again, were told of a long waiting list.

Then we went to the Coast Guard. The waiting list was even longer.

In desperation for action, we went to the Army. We were gung-ho and ready to go. Dennis' brother was in the Army, some of our friends had joined the Army, some had been drafted and now this seemed to be the place to go.

We walked into the recruiter's office and said, "We want to join the Army. We want to be infantry soldiers and go to Vietnam. How long will it take us to get in?"

The recruiter looked us in the eye and with a grin on his face replied, "How soon can you have your bags packed, boys?"

Right then and there we signed up on the *buddy plan* and we were ecstatic. The buddy plan meant that Dennis and I would get to go through basic and advanced training together and would be there to support each other through difficult times. This plan made joining the military a lot less intimidating and we expected to spend the first year of our military career working together.

The Physical

The recruiter told us it would actually take about two weeks to process the paperwork, get physicals and schedule us for induction. This was fine. It would give us time to party and say good-bye to our friends and families.

He scheduled us to go to downtown Los Angeles two days later to get physicals at the Army induction station with all the other enlistees and draftees.

The Army put us up in a sleazy hotel in the bad part of downtown L.A. the night before the physical so we could get there bright and early in the morning. Our room was on the eighth floor and had a lot of water damage on the ceiling and some of the walls. Since the hotel had fourteen floors, I assumed it wasn't from a leaky roof and later asked a clerk about it.

The clerk smiled and told us that a fire had burned some of the upper floors and the smoke and water damage made all floors above the eighth unusable. He assured me that the hotel was structurally sound, but it gave me an uneasy feeling.

After we checked in, it was time for dinner. We were expecting to get to eat in the hotel restaurant. What a laugh! We were sent to the "dining hall," which was nothing more than a few long tables stuffed behind a plywood partition on the far side of the hotel lobby.

There was no menu, just the meal d'jour. The dinner entree started out with a brown-tinged lettuce salad followed by scorched liver with onions and soggy succotash, all served on questionably clean, chipped and stained, white plates. Even the water tasted bad in this place! I think they were trying to prepare us for the food we would get in the Army. We ate only a few bites of our meal and decided to go down the street for a hamburger and fries.

I didn't sleep much that night. I was sure the place was full of rats and cockroaches and I didn't want *anything* crawling on me in the middle of the night.

We got up at 5:00 a.m. and went down to a breakfast that consisted of bitter coffee, powdered eggs and two strips of greasy leather I think were supposed to be bacon. Needless to say we didn't eat much and there wasn't time to go out and get anything else since we had to be at the induction center by six.

We got our first real taste of Army life the moment we arrived at the induction center. Everything was very tight. People in uniform spoke very concisely. There was no wasted effort.

We began by filling out reams of paperwork and taking psychological tests. We then were instructed to strip down to our underwear and proceed to the numbered stations. At each station we were instructed precisely what to do.

When we got to the part where they took blood pressure, mine was a little high. A young man in uniform led me to a small room that had a photomural of a beautiful stream running over rocks and through a lush green forest. I was instructed to lie down on the padded exam table that was against the wall and relax.

A few minutes later, a tall, blond woman dressed in civilian clothes came into the room and spoke very softly. She told me to look at the picture of the stream and to think of how peaceful it would be to be in that place.

I was just about to drift off to sleep when she put on the cuff and retested my blood pressure. "OK, you're normal, now get back in line!" She was suddenly abrupt and I was jerked back to reality and jumped off the table and out the door.

Everything else went pretty smoothly. After seven hours of being poked, probed, examined, tested and lectured to, we were informed that we had passed the physical exam and were approved for service in the armed forces. They said the recruiter would let us know what day to report back to be sworn in and processed to our training station.

Trouble With Oranges

A couple of days after the physical, Dennis and I were visiting with friends, Daryl and Jim. Jim was Daryl's older brother by adoption. We were celebrating our last days of freedom. Jim had been in the Army for about a year and was home on leave and we thought he might be able to give us some insight into Army life. It was around noon and we had been talking about the Army for a while but Jim wasn't much of a conversationalist so we decided to go for a drive in Daryl's VW Bug.

We piled into the Bug and went up to the hills to listen to music and talk. Daryl took us up a dirt road that went over the hills and came out in Chino, a small rural community south of where we lived in Orange County. We had never been up that road and were curious about what was up there.

Halfway over we decided to get out and stretch our legs and take a little walk. There wasn't much up there and we hadn't brought any food or drink with us so we didn't walk long before getting back in the car heading out.

Daryl thought it might be closer to go over the hill into Chino to get some food rather than go back toward home. Since we were hungry, we agreed that the sooner we got back to civilization the better.

The trip to Chino took longer than expected. By the time we got off the dirt road and out of the hills we were very hungry.

The first place we came to was a Sunkist orange grove. (There are many orange groves in this part of Southern California.) We saw folks picking oranges and thought oranges would quench our thirst and fill our bellies at the same time.

When we saw a good place to pull off the road, we jumped out and grabbed a few oranges off the trees. Since we had seen others out picking the oranges, we felt sure it would all right to take just a few.

After each grabbing an orange or two, we jumped back in the car and headed into town. Pulling away from the orange groves, Daryl noticed a pickup truck following us. He mentioned it had been parked near where we had picked the oranges.

I told Daryl to get on the freeway in case this guy was a local looking for trouble. I figured if he were looking for someone to fight with, he wouldn't bother following us onto the freeway. Daryl said he was still behind us after we pulled onto the freeway.

Suddenly there were two highway patrol cars beside us with their lights on, motioning for us to pull to the side of the road. I thought to myself, "What the hell is going on now?"

We pulled to the side of the road and were immediately handcuffed and placed under arrest. The highway patrol officers informed us of our rights and told us we were being arrested for stealing oranges out of the orange grove.

Little did we know there was a ring of people out stealing oranges from the groves and selling them elsewhere. The Sunkist growers had put guards in the groves to catch these thieves and we had the misfortune of picking a couple of oranges in front of one of these guards.

We had a hard time taking this seriously since we had taken only six oranges total and were driving a VW Bug. We had absolutely no place to put a large quantity of oranges if we were going to haul them off to market.

The Sunkist Growers Association decided to make an example of us and we were promptly hauled off to the local jail and charged with petty theft and trespassing. We were astounded.

When the arresting officer asked if we would post bail or stay in jail until the trial, we laughed and said, "We'll post bail. How much can it be?" We all had jobs and had been working up to that point and probably had several hundred dollars in cash between the four of us.

When the officer said, " Three hundred fifty dollars!" we started digging through our pockets. Then he looked at us and said in a cool voice, "Each."

Well, we didn't have that kind of cash on us and we said we would stay in jail until trial. At that point we figured we'd better use our one phone call to notify our families and let them know where we were.

We each called home and talked to our moms but, a few hours later, it was our dads who showed-up at the jail. I thought they would bail us out and give us a lecture and we would be home in our own beds by ten p.m.

No way. They decided we needed to be taught a lesson and figured a couple of days in jail wouldn't hurt us.

The cops in the jail were pretty nice and most of them thought the whole thing was pretty funny. We had each been placed in separate cells so we couldn't see each other. The cells were sparse with only a stainless steel toilet and a hard bunk hanging from the wall.

Jim and Daryl were in cells directly behind Dennis and me, separated by a block wall, but we could hear them if we listened at the heat register. There was also a block wall between my cell and Dennis' cell. Jim was a very sensitive fella and we didn't hear much from him.

Late that night they started bringing in the local drunks and throwing them in the drunk tank. The tank was an empty concrete cell at the end of the block next to Dennis with walls, ceiling and floor painted off white. There was a drain in the middle of the floor so it could be hosed down in the mornings.

The drunks moaned and threw-up all night long. Needless to say, we didn't get much sleep that night.

The next morning the jailor came to us and said blandly, "What do ya want fer breakfast?"

Being the wiseasses we were, we said, " Steak and eggs, hash browns, pancakes and coffee," figuring we would be lucky to get a bowl of mush.

The jailor walked away and about an hour later came back with everything we had ordered. We were sure it was some kind of mistake so we didn't say a word and ate it quickly before they found out.

Dennis and I decided if they asked us what we wanted for lunch, we would ask for hamburgers, fries and chocolate shakes.

When the jailor came and asked what we wanted for lunch we gave him our order. Sure enough, an hour later he brought everything we ordered.

I asked Dennis, "What kind of jail is this? They give us whatever we want to eat."

Dennis said, "Let's ask the jailor when he comes back."

When the jailor returned, I asked, " How come we get such good food in this place? I thought jail food was supposed to be bad."

The jailor replied, "We don't have a kitchen so we just get whatever ya want at the Denny's 'cross the street," and he walked away. This was turning out to be quite an interesting stay.

Later that evening I wondered how Jim was doing. We hadn't heard a word from him since we were locked up. Daryl said he hadn't been able to get him to talk so Dennis and I stood on our toilets and started talking to him through the heat register.

I knew Jim was worried that he might get in trouble with the Army for being arrested while on leave. I asked him about that and still got no answer.

Dennis and I gave up trying to talk to Jim and were lying on our bunks when we heard some rustling in Jim's cell. We both got up to the register and tried to get his attention. Jim made a few loud grunts and then the toilet flushed.

When the water stopped running, all was silent again. He was still not responding to us so I called the jailor and said, "I think Jim tried to flush himself down the toilet. Would you go check on him?"

The jailor returned in a few minutes and said, " He's doin' just fine, sittin' quietly on his bunk."

We never did hear a word from Jim.

The next day, after a fine breakfast, we went to court and pled guilty to stealing oranges from the grove. We told the judge how sorry we were and told him the story of our ride over the hill and our impending induction into the Army.

We expected to get a slap on the hand and be sent home but the judge felt he needed to set a precedent. He fined us $5,000 each and sentenced us to six months in jail.

He let us stand there silently with our mouths open for a while before he said he would suspend the fine and jail time if we'd write a five-thousand-word essay on petty theft and trespassing.

He then assured us this would go on our record.

The Power of the Army

We were a little worried because the Army recruiter said we couldn't have a criminal record and join the Army. We went down to the recruiting office and explained the whole story.

The recruiting sergeant said, " This isn't good, boys, but let's see what the power of the Army can do to straighten things out."

The next day the sergeant called and told me, "Everything has been fixed, son."

Dennis got a similar call and the deal was sealed. We were destined to become soldiers.

The Army had somehow gotten our records expunged and there were no more charges to worry about and no essays to write. I didn't question this action but accepted that the Army had enough clout to get the court to drop the whole thing.

For just a moment I thought about how much power the Federal Government wields and how they use it, but I quickly let it go, not really wanting to know.

Chapter 2

As the plane bumped to a landing in Bakersfield, my head snapped up. I cut my reminiscence short. Looking out the window of the small plane there wasn't much to see, just a few scruffy-looking palm trees and a lot of dust.

After we came to a stop at the terminal, a lone passenger got on the plane. He carried a black leather sample case and looked like a salesman in his dark blue, travel-worn suit. I was relieved when he found a seat near the front of the plane, leaving the seat next to me vacant.

When the plane taxied back to the runway, I made myself comfortable and drifted back to my daydream…

In the Army Now

Less than a week after we were arrested for stealing oranges from the orange grove, we were sworn into the Army at the induction center in L.A. and loaded on a bus bound for basic training at Ford Ord, California. We were on our way to becoming soldiers!

Dennis and I wiled away the seven-hour bus ride by chatting casually without addressing the fear and anxiety we both were feeling about our pending arrival at Fort Ord. I had heard many stories about how the drill sergeants would come onto the bus as soon as we arrived at the reception center and scream and yell at us to get off their bus. I heard that no matter how fast we piled out of the bus, it would not be fast enough. I had also heard we would be verbally assaulted and would have to do push-ups until we were completely unable to push ourselves up any more.

About a half hour before we were scheduled to pass through the gates of Fort Ord, I finally asked Dennis if he was feeling any fear about arriving at the reception center. I let him know my stomach was in knots and I felt like I might pass out from the anxiety of facing what was about to come. He admitted to being a little on edge himself. We rode the final few miles in silence and when the bus came to a stop at the Army reception center, we were not disappointed.

It was just after dark on March 15, 1968 when we passed through the front gates of the Fort Ord Army Training Center. Within a few minutes we arrived at the reception station.

The bus had barely come to a stop when a burley, young buck-sergeant jumped on board and started screaming commands. "Get off my bus, you maggots…You have one second to fall in at attention or you will be doing push-ups for the remainder of the evening."

The sergeant screamed and yelled and made us do push-ups while we tried to scramble into an acceptable formation. Nothing we did was right and the sergeant kept screaming at us and making us do push-ups.

Little did I know that from that moment on, my life would be forever changed. The first thing that began to fade was my innocence. Originally, I thought Army training might be nothing more difficult than high school football practice. Ha! From this perspective Army training was going to be hard physical work that made football practice seem like a picnic.

After the sergeant finished screaming at us, he led us inside a building and made us fill out paperwork. He actually seemed like a real person once he stopped yelling commands.

When everyone was done with his paperwork, he marched us over to the mess hall. We were allowed fifteen minutes to eat a late dinner and be back in formation outside.

The next step was to be marched to our temporary barracks. The sergeant informed us that we would only be there for a day or two until we received our assignments to a basic training company.

The temporary barracks were simple, wooden, two-story buildings. Metal-framed bunk beds lined the walls and lockers sat at the head of each set of bunks. The barracks had been built during World War II to house troops in training. A new training facility had been built a few years before our arrival and the new barracks were modern, two-story high, concrete construction.

Dennis and I grabbed a bunk together, he on top and me on the bottom. The sergeant gruffly informed us we would be falling out for breakfast at 0600 hours and we were to be showered, dressed and ready to begin our busy first day in the Army. He also let us know in no uncertain terms that we were to keep the barracks spotlessly clean. Nothing was to be left out of the lockers and our beds were to be made each morning.

0600 hours seemed to come very shortly after I got to sleep and it was a rude awakening. The sergeant came in screaming at the top of his lungs, "Fall out of those bunks, you maggots…up and at 'em… I want you dressed and in formation in ten minutes."

In ten minutes we were all showered, dressed and standing in front of the barracks like good soldiers, except for Steve. Steve was a little inept at everything he tried to do. He was the last one out and the sergeant made him do push-ups. Since we all thought it was funny, the sergeant made all of us do push-ups.

By the time we got to the mess hall, my arms were sore and I was hungry enough to eat a bear. The food was a lot better than what we got at the hotel before our enlistment physical.

After breakfast we were marched to the barbershop for our haircuts. After haircuts, we started to look like soldiers, everyone with the same buzz-cut. I remember thinking how funny Dennis looked when he came out of the barbershop. We had both had long hair. Now we had none. I felt like I had just lost a good friend.

When I looked at all the guys with their stubbled heads, it dawned on me that the Army was taking away our individuality. There wasn't much time to think about this new revelation. As soon as the last guy walked out of the barbershop, the sergeant lined us up and marched us to the next station.

The issuing of uniforms followed haircuts. We were all given a duffle bag and marched through a long warehouse where men behind counters shoved clothing at us as we called out our sizes. If they didn't have our size, they gave us the next bigger or smaller size, depending on which was closest at hand. We got shirts, pants, underwear, socks, hats, coats and everything you could imagine a soldier would need to endure the elements. We also got other assorted gear like a canteen, mess kit, entrenching tool (shovel) and whatever else we would need to be living in the field and carrying out our soldierly duties.

At the final station we had to give back all our shirts so they could sew on the nametags. There was also a white tag sewn above the right shirt pocket which identified us as trainees.

When we got back to the barracks, we were each handed a large cardboard box and told to fill it with everything we brought with us from home, all of our civilian clothes and other personal items, except shaving gear and toothbrush.

As I sealed the box I thought, "This is it. I'm a soldier now and there is no turning back." Packing my personal things gave me a funny feeling, like building a barrier between who I was as a child and who I would become as a soldier.

Again I thought, "The Army is taking away my individuality. A soldier is only a cog in a very big machine. The person is of no value as an individual because an individual is expendable and there is always another to take his place..." There wasn't time to continue this line of thought. I had to have my box packed and ready for shipping in a few minutes.

That night the tension in the barracks was running high because we were going "up the hill" to our new Basic Training Company in the early morning.

I stood in front of the mirror in the latrine and admired myself in the stiff, new, olive green uniform. I was reminded of the first time I wore my colorful blue and gold football uniform in high school. I felt a strong sense of pride at being part of a team. I wondered what this uniform would look like in eight weeks at the end of basic training and what *I* would look like in eight weeks. I was completely in awe of this massive organization called the United States Army.

I quietly repacked my duffle bag and laid out my uniform so I could get dressed quickly in the morning. After saying good night to Dennis, I crawled in my bunk and tried to sleep but movies kept playing in my head. All those World War II movies I had watched as a kid had really had an impact on me. I was seeing the training sequences over and over in my mind. I tried to rest but the drill sergeants were screaming in my mind and I was developing a strong sense of fear for what was to come.

Up the Hill

Morning came at 0500 hours. Not God's morning, the Army's morning. I'm not sure if I slept or not. All I remember is the thudding of the sergeant's boots as he stormed into the barracks and started yelling at everyone to get up and fall-in in front of the building with all of our gear. I was dressed and out the door in less than a minute, my heart pounding in my chest and the adrenaline driving me at a manic pace. It was a little anti-climatic; once we were all out on the street in front of the barracks we were calmly marched to the mess hall for breakfast.

After breakfast we stood next to our gear in the street and waited for our assignments. Dennis and I were assigned to Headquarters Company and instructed to get on one of the trucks with a bunch of guys we had not seen before. The truck was called a "Cattle Truck," a large stake bed semi-trailer with benches running down each side and it looked like the kind of truck that hauls livestock. We felt like cattle as we were herded onto the truck.

The anxiety was building and I was wondering, "Am I going to be able to get off this truck fast enough... how many push-ups will I have to do today... will I survive this day?!"

As the truck started to pull away I looked at Dennis and we both said in unison, "Here we go!"

The truck ride only took about ten minutes and I could see why they called the training area, "The Hill." There wasn't a flat piece of ground anywhere. The two-story concrete and glass barracks were all built on the side of the hill with the buildings going lengthwise up the hill. Immaculately kept lawns extended about twenty feet from the walls to the paved streets surrounding each building.

When we pulled up in front of Headquarters Company, the truck had barely come to a complete stop before two crisply uniformed drill sergeants (also known as drill instructors or DIs) wearing Smokey the Bear hats charged forward and started hollering at us to get off their truck.

We scrambled to gather our duffle bags and disembark the truck. Of course, we weren't quick enough to satisfy the drill sergeants. Within a few minutes we were all doing push-ups and being berated by the DIs.

In total there were about one hundred twenty trainees dropped off at our company area. We were divided into four platoons of thirty men each. Dennis and I were assigned to the second platoon. We were all instructed to stand at attention in front of the barracks on the company street.

Our platoon was assigned a drill instructor, Sergeant Lackey, and a platoon leader, Lieutenant Ross. Sergeant Lackey immediately started getting in our faces and asking questions while the platoon leader stood out front and watched.

He asked questions like, "Are you Regular Army (enlisted) or were you drafted?" and "Why are you in the Army?" Besides asking questions, he found some way to ridicule each and every one of us.

In a very short period of time, I learned that the *buddy plan* was an automatic invitation to being razzed and teased throughout basic training and announcing to the drill instructors we wanted to be infantry soldiers was equivalent to kissing a hornet's nest. It had never crossed my mind that volunteering for the Army and asking to be in the infantry was viewed as an act of idiocy.

When we told the DI we were enlisted and on the buddy plan, he walked over to the platoon leader and said something to him that I was not able to hear. He then walked back to where Dennis and I were standing at attention.

The D.I. got right up in our faces and told us to hold our heavy duffle bags above our heads, run down the hill to where a truck was parked and check the truck for enemy spies. He then added, "I want you to sing, 'I want to be an airborn ranger, I want to live a life of danger,' while you are running down and back and I want to hear it loud and clear!"

We did it and we were exhausted by the time we ran back up the hill. Everyone that laughed or smiled while we were running and singing had to do push-ups. By the time we returned to formation most of the company was down on the ground in push-up position.

I was humiliated and thought we had made a huge mistake in joining the Army. Dennis and I were the only trainees in the company who were on the "Buddy Plan."

Our first day of basic training continued to be rough. They taught us how to stand in formation and how to march in unison. They taught us how to salute and how to address officers and non-commissioned officers and what the difference was. We learned that discipline was the key to Army training, that we were not to argue commands and that we had to follow orders exactly as we were told. All of this was done in a derogatory tone. We were made to feel that we were the scum of the earth and not fit to breath the same air as our DIs.

By the end of the day I was ready to fall into my bunk and sleep, but that was not going to happen. Once inside the barracks we were instructed never to step on the center aisle of the floor and to keep it polished to a glassy finish at all times. We were ordered to keep our personal area neat, clean and organized per the Army Handbook. We also were told that we were to have our boots and brass polished and make sure there were no loose threads on our uniforms before morning formation. All of this took several more hours and I was so exhausted that I wasn't sure if I could continue...but I did.

Training

Basic training was tough but I learned a lot. I learned to run, and run some more, and when I was exhausted, run some more. Although I'd been an athlete in high school, I did not have a body conducive to running. My short legs, stocky body and short arms did not lend themselves well to the type of physical activity that Army training demanded.

In addition to running, I learned grit. To grit my teeth, that is, while I learned to run faster, farther, and longer than anyone else in my unit. Even though it hurt like hell I had no intention of giving up. I was constantly taunted to quit, to give up and even to leave the Army.

No sir! I had never walked away from a challenge in my life (albeit, a short life!) and I certainly wasn't going to walk away from this. I was learning how to become a soldier and, I believed, a man!

In basic training, target practice is simple and safe. The target is stationery. You move up, take aim and shoot. Targets don't shoot back or move. You stab a dummy with the bayonet, the cloth rips and sawdust falls out. Big deal. It doesn't fight back...it just hangs there. It doesn't breath, it doesn't look at you and it doesn't scream or bleed or feel pain. Even when we fought each other with pugil sticks (long sticks that are heavily padded so you can essentially beat each other senseless without doing permanent damage), no one got seriously hurt. There were no surprises. Everything was carefully planned and the risks were minimal.

Nobody dies in training. No blood is spilled. Even in live-fire exercises where we fired weapons and had explosives going off all around us, it was mostly one way. No one was firing directly back at us, with the exception of a machine gun firing high overhead to simulate enemy fire, that's exactly what the whole experience was, a simulation. The drill instructors controlled all the shooting, detonation of explosives and attacks. It was all very safe.

The purpose of the training was to acclimate us to battlefield conditions, build confidence, learn focus and learn to be a well-disciplined soldier. The whole point was to learn to take orders without question and react to deadly situations. There is no time to think in combat, just react and follow orders.

I was learning my lessons well. I obeyed orders like a good soldier and I was starting to enjoy soldiering.

Boy Scouts and Hand Grenades

Mentally, I viewed basic training as a type of advanced Boy Scouts. Although much more rigorous, Army training was similar to the Boy Scouts in that we went hiking and camping, learned survival techniques and learned to be prepared for whatever difficulties we might face in military life.

I learned to fire guns in the Boy Scouts, so the promise of firing machine guns and grenade launchers produced a pinnacle of thrills. That made Army training much more exciting than the Boy Scouts. I quickly learned about the many different types of weapons and how to use them. I especially liked the live-fire combat exercises. They were challenging and I excelled at them.

Some of the verbal and physical abuse we experienced in the first weeks of training was letting up. As we got to know each other, the DIs got a little friendlier. It was during this time I entertained the thought of making a career out of the military.

The Army seemed to work like a well-oiled machine. Although we complained often, I think most of the guys were impressed with the way everything worked so smoothly. Every day was well planned. The training was rough and rugged and we were all very tired by the end of each day, but with all the harsh training there were surprisingly few mishaps or injuries.

There was also a feeling that each day we would be pushed to our limit and each new day would bring a new limit to be pushed to. We were getting into shape both physically and mentally and I liked the way it felt.

Army training was as demanding on the psyche as it was on the body. Those with strong minds excelled and those that were not able to cope with the mental abuse and psychological pressure struggled. I don't think this struggling went unnoticed. I think those who were not able to cope as well were later placed in military occupations that were less demanding than direct combat situations.

There was one guy in our platoon named Greg who was always struggling and the DIs liked to pick on him. Actually they liked to pick on everyone from time to time, but Greg seemed to take it more personally than most. He started to get angry about the training exercises and the attention he was getting from the DIs.

One day Greg got sick and had to be taken back to the barracks for rest. No one knew it but he had pocketed a live round from the rifle range the day before and was planning to shoot one of the DIs.

When Greg was taken back to the barracks, he put his rifle in the rack at the front of our dormitory but didn't lock the rack. Later, when no one was around, he got his rifle out, loaded the live round into the chamber and stood by the second floor window waiting for a likely target.

Sergeant Diaz, one of the senior drill instructors, was coming in early from the training exercise to check on Greg. As he walked up the company street, Greg stuck his rifle out the window and fired his one and only bullet at Sergeant Diaz.

Fortunately for the sergeant, Greg was a poor shot and missed completely. Several people heard the shot and came running to help. The last I heard, they took Greg to a mental institution and discharged him from the Army.

I never learned anything more about poor Greg. He just wasn't able to cope with the high stress of Army training. I think there were several others who were also having difficulty, but were able to keep their emotions in check better than Greg.

By the end of the eight weeks of training, I was proud of being one of the toughest guys in the unit. Physically tough, but with a Boy Scout mentality; I was *playing* war. In the training war, people who were shot got up after counting to ten. There were no real casualties and no feelings about killing your enemy.

After eight weeks of extremely hard work, Basic Training was coming to an end and we were all feeling like we had accomplished a great deal. I felt good about myself and was in excellent physical and mental condition. I was looking forward to the next challenge. My mind and body were that of a warrior and I was beginning to have strong feelings about manhood and what that would mean. I was confident I could tackle any challenge and be victorious.

On the day we graduated from basic training there was going to be a big ceremony on the parade field and family and friends were invited to attend. I was looking forward to wearing my dress uniform and marching in front of the crowd, showing my pride at what I had accomplished. My family and several of my friends were planning to be there. On the morning of graduation, at breakfast formation, I was called out and told to report to the administration office.

When I got to the administration office, I was informed I would be boarding a plane at 0900 hours the next day bound for Fort Lewis, Washington. They said I needed to get my medical records updated and have orders cut to go to Fort Lewis. I spent the rest of the day at the Admin Center and had to miss the graduation ceremony. I was very disappointed because I wanted my friends and family to see me marching with my unit, wearing my dress-green uniform.

Since many of the guys in my unit were also going to be infantrymen, I had hoped we would be together for our advanced training. Not a chance. I was the only one from my unit assigned to go to Fort Lewis.

After graduation there was a big party and I was finally able to wear my dress uniform and spend some time with my family and friends. The party lasted well into the night. By the time I said my good-byes and returned to the barracks to pack my things for the trip to Washington the next morning, I was thoroughly exhausted.

No More Buddy Plan

The end of basic training also ended the buddy plan. The promise that Dennis and I would stay together during all of our training assignments was promptly broken. I was sent directly to Fort Lewis, Washington (near Seattle), to begin advanced infantry training. Dennis was a given a week's leave before being sent to some other Army post halfway across the country. That was the last time that I saw Dennis during my military career, my first awakening to the fact that the Army was not always honest and forthright in its dealings.

I went to advanced training alone. I felt I had suffered a great loss because I had developed a brotherly closeness with the guys from my training unit. Now I was facing a whole new experience with a whole new bunch of guys. To make matters worse, these guys in my new training unit had all been together since they were inducted into the Army. They were a family and *I* felt like an outsider.

Advanced Infantry Training, or AIT as it is most often called, was much like basic training except it was more intense, focused more on fighting and killing the enemy and focused less on military protocol. I excelled at map reading and escape and evasion exercises and enjoyed the night-fire exercises with the bright red tracer bullets flying through the darkness.

Throughout the eight weeks of advanced training I managed to make a couple of friends. For the most part, however, I remained a loner and never really fit in with the main group.

The training itself proved slightly more difficult for me, not because of physical demands or challenges, but because it began to dawn on me what we were being trained for. I was starting to go beyond my Boy Scout mentality to the realization we weren't going to kill "dummies" or just shoot at "targets." I was now starting to understand I would be shooting at real people and, perhaps more importantly, real people would be shooting at me with *real* bullets, fully intent on killing *me*.

Wake-up, Manchild

When AIT was finished, most of the guys got orders to go to their next duty station. A handful of us, including myself, were held for an additional week of training before receiving our orders. It was clear where we were being prepped to go. This additional training was entirely focused on the specifics of fighting the ground war in Vietnam. We learned to detect booby traps, understand the Vietnamese culture and fight the guerilla war. There was little doubt that we would be getting orders to go fight the war in Vietnam.

I was not surprised when I finally got my orders to go to Vietnam, but still, I had only an inkling of the reality of war. The horror, the evil, the violence, the blood, guts and death of war are so far removed from living and training in the U.S. it was impossible to fully grasp the effect of that experience without being there. I had my orders and I clung tightly to my ideals.

I was still clinging to a little piece of the Boy Scout in me. I believed with all my heart that I could just go to Vietnam, fight the war just like we did it in training, come back and I'd be a hero. I would be respected. I would be a man.

As an eighteen-year-old, I also believed that having a foreign adventure was part of being a man and being a soldier. I dreamed of beautiful foreign women, of being thousands of miles away from home and experiencing new and exotic things. It was all supposed to be a part of the rite of passage, of becoming a man.

The Final John Wayne Movie

Having grown up with a Boy Scout/John Wayne mentality, I had no reference point for how soldiers dealt with the realities of war and death. In the movies, when John Wayne shot someone, it wasn't real. Everyone knew the actor was just acting and would get up after the cameras stopped. The movies portrayed war and military service as an honorable quest. Dying a hero's death in battle was held in high esteem. I was greatly influenced by this type of portrayal. It never occurred to me how traumatic it would be to shoot at a real person or how horrific it would be when I saw my friends die. I never imagined that the effects of war would torment me emotionally and physically for the rest of my life.

After I finally graduated from AIT, I was given a week's leave before I was to report to the replacement depot in Oakland, California. From there I would be shipped to Vietnam to practice my trade as a soldier.

My plane was not leaving until the next day so, before leaving to go home, I went to the post movie theater and saw the new John Wayne movie about the Vietnam war, "Green Beret." I guess it was fitting that the last movie I would see before going to war was John Wayne's Hollywoodization of the Vietnam War.

The trip from Seattle to Los Angeles was uneventful. Although I wore civilian clothes, my haircut and demeanor gave me that military "look." No one got too close to me.

My family met me at the airport and I spent the next week going out with friends and partying. I really didn't know how much to tell my friends about my Army training. They all knew where I was going and they didn't bring it up much.

The Last Kiss Goodbye

On the final night of my leave, I went out for pizza with a group of my friends. Shelly, one of the girls from the group of high school kids I hung around with, was at the pizza party and paying a lot of attention to me. We had never really dated but she had always been one of the girls that hung close to me when we would go out as a group. I liked girls a lot and the girls seemed to like me, but I was shy and never had a steady girlfriend in high school.

After the pizza party, Shelly approached me and asked if I would drive her home. She scooted into the front seat of my dad's Ford Country Squire station wagon and, to my surprise, slid across the bench seat to sit next to me. I was a little scared so I tried to act cool and carry on a casual conversation as I drove her home to her parent's house.

When I pulled up in the driveway, I shut the engine off and turned out the headlights because it was after 11:00 p.m. and I didn't want to wake her parents or the neighbors. I had just turned out the lights when Shelly threw her arms around me and gave me a great, big, wet kiss.

I had kissed girls like this before, but there was something different about this kiss, something more intimate. I didn't want any involvements before going off to war so I gently broke off the kiss and told Shelly I would see her at the airport in the morning.

When she got out of the car she had a big smile on her face and said, "See you in the morning… honey."

Chapter 3

The Road to War

When the little turbo-prop touched down in Oakland, I was having warm thoughts about that kiss from Shelly the night before. I pulled myself together and stood up to exit the plane.

I was the last person off and when I stepped down on the tarmac, I felt lonely. I was going off to war all by myself. No buddy was going with me to share the experience. Everyone with whom I came in contact was a stranger. I felt no sense of comfort or familiarity anywhere. Although it was a warm summer day, Oakland felt like a very cold place.

It was a twenty-minute taxi ride to the replacement depot and when I got there I was pleasantly surprised. The compound was semi-secluded with neat little red brick buildings, perfectly manicured lawns and flower gardens and a few nicely placed trees. It was quite a contrast to the ugly gray of the big city.

I was placed in a room with four single-tier bunks. No one occupied the other three bunks yet, so I had my choice of where to sleep and I chose the corner farthest from the door. There were wall lockers between the bunks that created a partition, giving the corner bunk a feeling of seclusion and safety.

The corporal who signed me in and showed me to my room was quite pleasant and gave me a quick briefing before he left. He informed me I would be there for a couple of days and the uniform of the day was duty fatigues. All personnel were expected to be out of bed and dressed no later than 0600. We were to fall into formation in the street outside the mess hall after breakfast and lunch. Then the duty sergeant would call out the names of the men to be sent to the staging area. I had already missed lunch so I wouldn't have to worry about that until the next day. It all seemed much more informal than my training experiences and certainly moved at a much slower pace.

The food was good and the place was quite peaceful and calm. It didn't seem like a military base, even though it was surrounded by a tall brick wall and had lots of armed guards to ensure that no unauthorized persons got in *or* out. It was clear we were being held in a very secure location.

The other three guys showed up in my room late in the day and we all introduced ourselves, but I don't think anyone paid much attention to names. By this time we had all learned how to remain detached from interpersonal relationships while giving the impression of being interested.

I learned in training that each time I would form bonds with guys in my unit I would eventually be separated from them. Because I was young and separated from family and friends I tended to bond quickly. These separations were painful and I really didn't want to get to know someone for a day or two and then never see them again. Because Vietnam was a one-year duty station I knew I would probably make some close friends there. I had no idea how deeply impacted I would be by the separations and losses I would experience in the war zone.

The next morning after breakfast we were all standing in the street waiting for someone to come out and call us to attention when a tall, skinny sergeant and a short, pudgy-faced corporal emerged from a door near the mess hall.

As the corporal approached, he screamed, "Ten hut!" As we all snapped to attention, a deuce-and-a-half (that's what the Army called a two-and-a-half ton truck used for hauling just about anything, including troops) pulled up to our left.

The sergeant said in a calm voice, "At ease, men. When your name is called, you will get your gear, strip your bunk and make sure your quarters are as clean as they were when you arrived. After I have finished calling names, those whose names were called will have ten minutes to complete their duties and be on that truck."

When the sergeant finished calling names, he turned and calmly walked back to the door from which he had emerged. The corporal watched him walk away, then turned to us and yelled in his best command voice, "Dismissed!"

My name wasn't called at the breakfast formation and the procedure was followed exactly the same after lunch. Again my name was not called.

I was getting a little nervous about where the deuce-and-a-half was taking the guys whose names had been called. I asked around but nobody had any information about what was happening, nor did they seem to know exactly where the staging area was. The regular personnel seemed to be exceedingly tight-lipped about the processing procedures, as if they were some kind of national secret.

Everyone was staying to themselves and I was in no hurry to make new friends in this very temporary situation. I didn't know where that truck was taking people, but I figured I would find out soon enough. I found a comfortable place to sit and read a book while waiting out the evening.

The next morning after breakfast I was hoping my name would be called. No such luck. I was getting pretty antsy hanging around reading. I was anxious to get to the staging area, even though that meant getting closer to the war.

I started thinking about what it would be like to fight and die in the war. I wondered how my friends and family would react to the news of my death if I were killed. I wondered what death would be like and if it would be a long, painful process or a quick flash and then nothing. Was there any kind of afterlife? I wanted to believe that there was a spirit that would live on after I was dead, but I wasn't absolutely sure that there was a spirit at all.

However, I realized I couldn't afford any more thoughts about death. I had to stay focused on the present and surviving through the next year. One last thought quickly moved through my head as I tried to shift my thinking, "Will I be alive to see my nineteenth birthday, four months from now?"

I went to the day room to read but couldn't stop thinking about what might happen in the war. I felt that if I was going to die I would like it to be quick and the last thing I wanted was to return home maimed. I thought at that point I would much rather die than be crippled for the rest of my life.

Finally, my name was called at the after-lunch formation. When the corporal dismissed us, I rushed to my room to gather my gear and get on the truck. I stripped the sheets off my bunk, threw them in the laundry and folded the blanket neatly at the foot of the bare mattress. I quickly mopped the floor and made sure everything was exactly as I had found it.

When I got to the truck there were only two of the fifteen or so who had been called but I could see the others coming from different directions.

Within a few minutes we were all on the truck. An armed MP (military policeman) jumped on the back of the truck as the tailgate went up. The MP was carrying an M-16 rifle and didn't smile or make eye contact with anyone. He sat stoically as the sergeant came and called the names one last time to make sure everyone who was supposed to be on the truck was there.

As the truck began to move I looked at the MP. He had a sadistic little grin forming on his face as if to say, "I'm glad you are going there and not me."

The Staging Area

The deuce-and-a-half took us a couple blocks toward the rear of the compound and through a guarded gate. The staging area was an extremely sterile place with a very large, windowless, concrete building surrounded by a wide asphalt road. It was enclosed by a concrete block wall topped with barbed wire. We were taken to the backside of the building where I saw several large, roll-up doors and several smaller entry doors. The truck stopped near an entry door at the far end of the concrete building.

The MP who had been riding with us jumped off the back of the truck and waited by the door. No one on the truck moved a muscle.

While we waited, the door opened and another MP, wearing a sidearm, stepped out and walked to the back of the truck. He calmly said, "Okay, men, step off the truck in single file, walk through the door and have a seat to your left."

When I walked through the door, I could see this was just a big, open warehouse with a few areas divided off by temporary partitions and maybe a few rooms at the far end. To my left were a couple rows of folding chairs sitting in front of an empty table. There was a buzz of people talking but it was hard to hear anything specific as the echoes bounced off the concrete walls.

I took a seat in the first row of chairs and sat quietly. This place felt cold and inhumane.

The MP that rode in the deuce-and-a-half with us did not enter the building and the side-armed MP quickly stepped inside and closed the door. He walked up to the empty table, surveyed his audience and began speaking.

"Gentlemen, you are all currently under orders to report for duty in the Republic of Vietnam. This is the staging area where you will be issued all your basic combat gear and uniforms. You will remain here until you are called to go to the airport and board your plane. Prior to your departure you will be briefed about the procedures you are to follow. You will be issued your Geneva Convention Card just prior to departure and sworn to uphold the Geneva Convention. Your Geneva Convention Card is your 'license to kill' and you will be held under armed guard until you board the airplane on your way to the Republic of Vietnam. Are there any questions?"

No one spoke. I think we were all in shock. The MP didn't wait long for questions before telling us to rise and follow him to the waiting area.

The waiting area was about forty square feet surrounded by a black curtain with a six-foot opening in the front. It had bunks neatly arranged in rows. Each bunk had a blanket, mattress and pillow but no sheets.

The MP informed us that there were no assigned bunks. We would only come here to rest when we were not otherwise occupied. I got the distinct impression we would not be sleeping much and that we would not be here long.

A couple of the guys had buddied-up and were talking to each other by their bunks but I stayed to myself as did most of the rest. Everything here was so uncertain that I felt more comfortable keeping to myself and carrying on small talk only when necessary.

Before we could set our bags down and get comfortable, a tall, slim, bespectacled Spec. 4 (a Spec. 4 was an E-4 specialist, similar to the rank of corporal) with a clipboard in hand came in and ordered us to move. He instructed us to pick up our duffle bags and go to the clothing station.

The clothing station, which was on the other side of the building, was much like the clothing issue station in basic training. There were long lines of boxes full of uniforms and gear. The station was manned by tired looking enlisted men who seemed to care less whether we got the right sizes or not.

The Spec. 4 stood behind an empty table. He told us to line up single file. He instructed us each, in turn, to dump the contents of our bag on the table so he could inspect our gear.

When I dumped my bag out on the table, he pointed out what I was allowed to keep and confiscated the rest.

We were each allowed to keep our khaki travel uniform, one set of clean underwear and our shaving gear. After taking all my fatigues and unnecessary items, the specialist handed me my duffle bag and a checklist of items I would need to have in it before leaving the area.

The checklist looked like a list of the same gear we got in basic training except for the jungle fatigues. I was excited about getting to wear the jungle uniform. It was like a badge of honor. I was still proud to be serving my country. Thinking about wearing the combat clothes made me feel honored to be a soldier.

We were issued several sets of lightweight, loose fitting, cargo-pocketed jungle fatigues and an ample supply of Army green underwear and socks. We got a mess kit, canteen, backpack and other assorted gear, everything needed to survive in combat except a gun and ammunition. I had to stop several times to reorganize my duffle bag so everything would fit without bulging.

It took several hours to go through the maze of issue stations, hurrying here, waiting in line there. At the final station, a lively looking Spec. 4 instructed me to put on my khaki travel uniform and turn in the stateside fatigues I was wearing.

I went to the waiting area to change and found there were several others doing the same. I sensed it was getting close to the time we would go to the airport and begin the journey to the war zone. The tension in my gut was beginning to rise and I could feel the fear crawling up my spine.

I wondered when we would be issued weapons. I thought it would be a strange feeling to walk around with a loaded weapon. In training we often carried our rifles but were never allowed to have live ammunition except at the rifle range and then only when we were on the firing line.

I didn't have time to think much more about it. I think that is why we were kept so busy, so we wouldn't have much time to think.

When I turned in the last bit of my stateside gear, I suddenly realized, "I'm not a trainee anymore; I'm a real soldier getting ready for combat." I wasn't sure what being a "real soldier" actually meant but it felt good at the time.

The PFC (private first class) who took my clothes handed me a small stack of papers, pointed me to some partitions at the far side of the building and told me to report there immediately. The papers were medical forms so I knew I was in for another round of inoculations.

Sure enough, I went through the partition and there were the white-coated medicos ready to probe, jab and inspect every part of my body once again. After they finished the physical exam and the inoculations, I was feeling a little dizzy and nauseated. The medic told me to go to the waiting area and lie down for a while. I fell asleep as soon as I hit the bunk and slept for several hours. When I awoke I realized we had been in processing most of the night and it was now 0600 hours, morning again.

I walked over to the mess area to get some breakfast. I was famished and felt like I hadn't eaten in days. After eating, I was walking back to the waiting area when a corporal came up and said, "Make sure you are back in the waiting area by 0700."

I went straight back to the waiting area. In a few minutes we were all called to report to the briefing room which was the only area in the building that had permanent walls.

I walked into the briefing room and took a seat near the back in the third of four rows of folding chairs. A staff sergeant entered from a door near the front of the room carrying a black satchel. I knew immediately this was where we would get our Geneva Convention Card, our license to kill.

The sergeant quickly issued the cards, briefed us and made us swear we would uphold the articles of the Geneva Convention. Even after the briefing I wasn't sure what the Geneva Convention was, exactly why we had to be sworn to uphold it or why I needed a "license to kill" in a war zone. All I knew for sure was that I now had everything I needed to go to war except a gun and it wouldn't be long before I was loaded on a plane bound for the Republic of Vietnam.

The Bizarre Flight to War

Before we left the briefing area an armed MP joined us. He instructed us to have all our gear ready to go in five minutes. The MP said he would follow us to the waiting area and then lead us to our bus.

When we were ready, the MP told us to stack our duffle bags outside the waiting area where they would be transported to the airport and loaded on the plane. We were led out the same door through which we had entered the building the day before and marched on to a waiting, olive green, Army bus.

There was another armed MP already on the bus. I felt like the Army was taking a lot of precautions to ensure we didn't become deserters. I wondered if I should be more fearful than I already was.

After the last person was aboard, the first MP got on and sat in front near the driver. The bus took us to an airport. I'm not sure if it was a civilian airport or military airport, but we were certainly *not* taken to the main passenger terminal. It looked like some kind of cargo terminal.

The MPs marched us off the bus in double file. They led us through the small terminal and out onto the tarmac. The plane, a large silver bird with the words "Flying Tiger" written on the side, was waiting for us. But before we could board, a coverall-clad man came up to the MP and excitedly notified him there was a mechanical problem with the plane. He said we could not get on board yet. This was clearly not standard operating procedure because the MP was unsure about what to do with us while we waited for the airplane to be readied.

We were quickly herded back inside the terminal building and lined up against a wall. The MP said the plane needed a quick repair and told us we would have to sit there on the floor until it was ready to go.

We all sat down on the floor and it felt like we were prisoners being held for the gallows. The MPs stood and watched us until the same coverall-clad man came back. He told the MP that the plane was ready to go and we could now be loaded.

We entered the plane through a door near the back of the wing where a portable gangway had been moved into place. The interior of the plane was simple, with no overhead baggage compartments and no-frills seating. There were two seats on each side of an aisle running the length of the plane.

Since there was plenty of room, we could sit with an empty seat next to us. Some of the guys paired up, but like before in the staging area, most stayed to themselves, including me.

I noticed the MPs did not board with us and we had been joined by two stewardesses (that's what they were called before they became known as flight attendants). The stewardesses announced that once we were in the air they would be serving meals and soft drinks until we reached Japan. They didn't say what would happen after we left Japan and no one asked.

I heard the engines start and the plane began to taxi to the runway. Suddenly we stopped. The pilot came over the intercom and said that there was a minor problem. He told us we would stay on board while someone came out to fix it.

It seemed like we were having a lot of problems getting this plane off the ground and I wondered if it would make it all the way to Vietnam in one piece.

We sat for about twenty minutes. Then I heard the engines start again and the pilot came on apologizing for the delay.

This time we made it to the runway and had a successful takeoff. I was nervous, but figured the Army wasn't about to let me die before I got to their little war in Vietnam.

As soon as we were at cruising altitude, the stewardesses came along and offered soft drinks and a box lunch. I had no sooner finished my box lunch than the pilot came on the intercom. He announced that the plane was again experiencing some mechanical difficulties. We were told we would have to land in Seattle to have it fixed and he assured us that we were in no danger. He said the problem was just part of a back-up system that was required to be operational while we were in flight.

Twenty minutes later we were on the ground in Seattle, rolling toward the passenger terminal. Since I had been here a little over a week ago, I felt some comfort in the fact that it was a familiar place.

When we came to a stop at the terminal, the stewardess informed us it would take about an hour and a half to make the repairs. She said we could get off the plane if we agreed to stay in the waiting area and not go into any of the bars. I was surprised they would let us off the plane without an armed guard.

As I was getting off, the guy who was sitting across the aisle asked me if I wanted to go to the lounge and get a drink. I looked at him incredulously and to my surprise said, "What the hell, sure! What are they gonna do, send us to Vietnam?"

We walked through the waiting area and found a cocktail lounge nearby. We walked into the lounge and sat at an empty spot at the bar. Before we had a chance to order, a couple of tough looking marines walked in and sat next to us. I thought, "Oh man, I hope these guys don't start any trouble."

The marine sitting next to me gave me a hard look and said, "What are you doggys doing in this place?"

I quickly told him we were on our way to Vietnam and the story of the plane trouble. He slapped me on the back and, to my shock, offered to buy us a round of drinks. We quickly became pals.

They told us they had just returned from Vietnam themselves and that they felt sorry for us. We all moved to a booth and the marines kept buying drinks until we were barely able to walk. They didn't want to talk about Vietnam and said we would learn soon enough.

We all had a good ol' time, and then realized we needed to get back to the plane so we didn't get in trouble. Since they had succeeded in their effort to get us drunk, the marines were kind enough to help us stagger back to our plane.

Once back on the plane, my new friend and I sat together and talked about how much fun it was to drink with the marines. In our intoxicated state we had let down our barriers and allowed ourselves to get close. I'm sure the stewardess could smell the booze on us, but she never said a word and brought us a couple of cokes. We weren't in the air more than ten minutes before the exasperated pilot announced we were still having mechanical difficulties. He said we would be making a short stop in Anchorage, Alaska.

I had never been to Alaska and thought it would be a great experience to be there. The alcohol had clouded my thoughts about where I was going and the trip was stretching into a bizarre expedition where the end was of no consequence. The only thing we were all wondering was, "Where will we land next?"

There wasn't much to see in Anchorage, just a long stretch of tarmac surrounded by some brownish piles of snow along the edge of the runway. There was also a small terminal with a lounge, a gift shop and a single counter that served all comers.

The cold, crisp Anchorage air felt good on my face. It helped to sober me a little from all the drinking I had done in

Seattle, but that wasn't going to stop me from having a drink here. This time several of the guys joined us in the lounge, but there was only time for one drink before the plane was fixed and ready to take to the air once more.

After we boarded the plane again, we went back to our separate seating arrangement and I settled in quietly. The pilot announced he thought we would be able to make it all the way to Japan now and didn't anticipate any more trouble. He also assured us that the plane was safe and all of the problems we had encountered were of a secondary nature. I felt like he was telling the truth so I pushed my seat back and tried to sleep off my intoxication.

The flight to Japan was quite smooth and there were no more breakdowns. I woke up from my nap just in time to see the soft glow of lights shining up from the Japanese coast. We were only stopping in Japan for a short time, but the stewardess said we could get off and stretch our legs.

When I stepped off the plane I was surprised that it was quite warm and humid in Japan. I wasn't expecting that, but I'm not sure what I was expecting. We had landed at a U.S. Air Force base in Yakuska, Japan.

There wasn't anything to see in the dark of the night. We were directed to step inside a small building where there were some wooden benches and a coffee pot. I had barely finished my first cup of coffee when a young PFC stuck his head in the door and told us it was time to reboard the plane.

I settled back in my seat for the final leg of this bizarre flight and a little chill ran up my back. I suddenly realized the stewardesses were not on the plane.

Just as I was beginning to feel the full impact of where we were going, I was jolted upright in my seat by the pilot's voice.

"You have probably noticed by now that all non-essential personnel have stayed behind for this last part of our journey. We will be landing in the Republic of Vietnam in about an hour and the plane will stay on the ground only long enough to unload passengers and cargo. We hope you have enjoyed our eventful flight. On behalf of the entire crew I would like to wish you all the best of luck on your current duty assignment."

It felt especially lonely without the stewardesses. I was once again feeling that I was all alone on this strange journey. I wondered if any of the guys on the plane would be going to the same unit as I was going to. I was wondering how soon we would be issued rifles. It was scary to think I would be getting off the plane in a hostile country with no way to protect myself.

I was becoming extremely fearful and anxious. I calmed myself by remembering that the Army would take care of me and tell me everything I needed to know when I needed to know it. I had faith in the Army.

When the plane was over Vietnam, I kept watch out the window to see if I could see any signs of the war. I could see some lights below when the pilot came on the intercom. He told us we were circling the landing zone at Bien Hoa Air Base. He also announced we would continue to circle for a few minutes more because there was a mortar attack north of the runway in our approach lane.

Now I was really scared. We were being shot at and we hadn't even touched ground yet. All kinds of thoughts went through my head. I had just spent a grueling eighteen hours getting here and I could be killed in the first few minutes after my arrival. I was wondering if we would have to run for cover as soon as we got off the plane. I really didn't know what to expect.

Finally, the plane touched down and taxied to the edge of the runway. It seemed like forever before they got the gangway into place.

When the door opened, I was immediately taken aback by the heat and humidity. It had been warm and humid in Japan, but it was definitely *hot* and humid here.

I started to think that the heat and humidity might kill me before the enemy ever had a chance. It was hard to breathe the hot, sticky air and the thought of being shot at as I stepped off the plane made me nauseous.

Chapter 4

It was late July 1968; I was just eighteen years old, still "wet behind the ears" as the saying goes. Mentally and physically the Army had toughened me into a man, but deep inside I was still a boy. I had never in my short life traveled outside of the United States. Yet here I was, in a state of shock, halfway around the world in the Republic of Vietnam.

I stepped off the plane and stood in the middle of the landing strip at two a.m. I was scared shitless. It was pitch black except for the soft glow of the lights surrounding the briefing area. I thought to myself, "Hey, we're exposed, they could shoot at us!"

I followed the others across the tarmac as they walked to the briefing area. I looked back and I could see some men unloading our duffle bags from the cargo hold of the plane.

The briefing area was a large concrete slab with a tin roof supported by steel poles. At the front of this structure there was a long table and a couple of metal folding chairs. Facing the front table were about a hundred folding chairs, all lined up in neat rows. Standing in front of the chairs was man in a neatly pressed uniform with sergeant stripes. He informed us we were to collect our duffle bags and wait there until the bus arrived to take us to our base camp.

As the sergeant spoke, I noticed several hundred large crates stacked out behind the briefing area. The crates were open on the sides and I could see each crate contained a shiny aluminum canister about six or seven feet long and nearly three feet in diameter. When the sergeant was done speaking I walked up to him and quietly asked, "What's in those canisters out back?"

He calmly looked me in the eyes and said, "Those are dead bodies waiting to be shipped home."

I suddenly got a huge knot in my stomach and felt extremely vulnerable. It wasn't until much later I found out the canisters actually contained bombs, not bodies. The sergeant had played a cruel trick on me.

I started to relax a bit when I noticed there were quite a few people walking around totally unconcerned about getting shot at, so I figured we must be in safe area.

My senses were very keen as I stood nervously waiting for the bus. The hot, damp air was full of unusual odors like musty wood smoke, dirty clothes, burning diesel fuel and rotting leaves. There were smells I could not identify and the thickness of the air made each aroma linger and blend with the next. I couldn't see much beyond the dimly lit briefing area and my mind ran rampant speculating what sights and sounds lay ahead.

The clattering of the bus shattered my thoughts as it pulled in near where I was standing and came to an abrupt stop. It was similar in color and size to the bus that had taken us to the airport in Oakland, but this bus was much dirtier and had heavy expanded-metal screens covering the glassless windows.

My heart pounded in my throat. I was drenched in sweat. My duffle bag felt like it weighed a ton as I dragged it through the door and up the steps of the bus. The bus driver appeared totally emotionless, as if this were an ordinary day in an ordinary place and he was driving us uptown to our morning job.

We rode over dusty, bumpy roads and through what seemed to be small villages. Someone had mentioned we were going to Long Bien. Sometime during training I had seen a map of Vietnam and I knew that Bien Hoa and Long Bien were located in the southern part of the country near Saigon, the capitol of South Vietnam.

We were clearly not on the military base and I felt quite vulnerable riding through these villages completely unarmed and unescorted. No one spoke during the entire trip and I was feeling isolated and detached. The entire experience from the time we left Oakland felt very surreal and I was having difficulty integrating myself into the reality of war.

A Pretty Good Soldier

When we arrived at Long Bien, it was still dark and I didn't fully comprehend the meaning of where I was or what I would be doing there. We were let off in front of a simple, tent-like building that had a canvas roof with wooden sides and a few screened windows on each side. A tired-looking staff sergeant stepped out of the building and motioned us through the door.

He blandly welcomed us to Vietnam, then told us we were now at the Long Bien replacement depot. We would be assigned to our field unit within a few days. He also informed us that while we were here we would have to pull duty. He said there would be a duty roster posted each morning notifying us when and where to report for duty.

As the sergeant droned on, I looked out the screened window to see a pink glow in the sky as the sun began to rise. I was surprised to see morning again. I realized I hadn't slept much since we left Oakland, and with all the stress of going to war, I was running out of adrenalin. My head was aching and my body felt like it was made of lead. I was too tired to be scared and too scared to be tired. What a dilemma!

The staff sergeant finished his boring lecture and took us outside to give us a tour of the camp. I was intrigued by the simple but functional wood and canvas construction of the barracks. They were similar to the first building we were in. There was a double row of two-story barracks with a concrete sidewalk down the middle and a trench on either side of the walkway. The sergeant said that in the event of a mortar attack we should leave the barracks and take cover in the trench.

He showed us the mess hall, supply tent, showers and the latrines (that's what the Army calls the toilet). There were two wooden, four-hole latrines, one for officers and one for enlisted men. The sergeant explained that they were to be used only for bowel movements.

He pointed to several large, plastic pipes that were sticking out of the ground at an angle with a piece of wire mesh secured over the opening. He said these were "piss tubes" and were to be used when we had to urinate. It then dawned on me there were no women on this base and thus, according to the Army, no need for privacy.

After the lesson on how to fulfill our need to eliminate, the sergeant finally dismissed us so we could go to the barracks to get some rest. He said to be sure to check the duty roster because some of us would have duty later in the day.

I figured I had better check the duty roster before I went to the barracks because I didn't want to get up one minute before I needed to.

The duty roster indicated I should report to the sergeant of the guards at 0500 hours the following day. That was great. It meant that I could sleep all day and would have some time in the evening to organize my gear.

I slept soundly until late afternoon and awoke with a burning hunger. I got dressed and walked to the mess hall to see if it was time for the evening meal.

When I arrived they were just starting to serve dinner so I quickly got in line.

I didn't bother asking what was being served. The meat looked like some kind of Swiss steak so I stuck my tray out and let them pile it full. There was meat, vegetables, potatoes and a little square of chocolate cake for dessert. I remember thinking, "Well, the food's not that bad, in fact, it's pretty darn good."

It wasn't until I had finished eating every morsel that I learned what I thought was poorly prepared Swiss steak was, in reality, liver and onions. Vietnam was full of surprises and I wasn't even in combat yet.

After dinner I ran into my drinking buddy from the bizarre flight. He told me there was an EM Club (Enlisted Men's Club) back behind the mess hall and wondered if I wanted to go get a drink. I quickly agreed.

Drinking was a great way to pass the time in the Army. I had learned to drink while in AIT. There was a beer hall down the street from our training unit. On the evenings when we didn't have duty we were allowed to go there and drink beer. You could get a pizza and a pitcher of beer for two bucks. That was a good buy since my salary while in training was only ninety dollars a month.

The EM Club was a small, wooden building with a few tables, a bar and a jukebox. I ordered a rum and coke and sat back thinking that back home I was not yet old enough to buy alcoholic beverages. Here it was okay though. I was a boy living in a man's world.

I went to bed thinking, "I've been here a whole day and I still don't have a gun. How am I supposed to defend myself if we come under attack?" I was too tired to think about it much and fell asleep, confident the Army would keep me safe.

Around 0200 (that's two o'clock in the morning) I was jolted from a sound sleep by a loud explosion and a bright flash of light. I could hear a lot of commotion outside as I raced out of the barracks and jumped into the trench.

Several more explosions followed and I clung to the bottom of the trench feeling like I needed to be much deeper. A few minutes passed without another explosion. Someone walked by and yelled, "All clear!"

As I stood up I noticed the front of my pants were all wet. I looked to see if there was any standing water in the trench. I was so scared I had peed my pants. I was embarrassed and quickly ran into the barracks to change my clothes.

Road Guard

At 0500 I reported to the sergeant of the guards. My first assigned combat duty was as a road guard. I was stationed at a crossroad just inside the main entrance to the base. They gave me an M-16 rifle and a hand radio, but no bullets for the rifle.

I was told if I thought I needed to shoot at something, I could contact the sergeant of the guards and he would come out, assess the situation and issue bullets if needed.

I felt foolish standing in the middle of the crossroad in the dark. What was I protecting with an unloaded rifle? I could see the main gate ahead about two hundred yards. It was manned by two armed MPs. I'm sure they had bullets for their guns.

There was a building twenty yards to my right and another twenty yards to my left. Each building had some activity, but I was unsure what was going on inside them.

As I stood trying to see something in the dimly lit buildings, two officers emerged from the building on my right and walked toward me. When they got close, I snapped to attention and gave them a crisp salute. They both casually returned my salute without making eye contact, walked passed me directly to the building on my left and promptly entered.

A few minutes later two more officers came out of the building on the right and walked past me to the other building.

Again, except for returning my salute, they made no acknowledgement I existed.

Soon there was a whole stream of officers walking to the building on my left and I saluted each one of them as they passed. I overheard one of them say, "What's for breakfast?" and another replied, "Probably the same as yesterday."

Bingo! I was guarding the road from the officer's quarters to the officer's mess. No wonder they didn't want me to have any bullets in my weapon, this was nothing more than busy work. I wasn't protecting a damn thing.

As day was breaking and the officers were chowing down, I was enjoying the scenery along the hills in front of me. While I watched the sun rise over the hills, I saw a flash of light and a puff of smoke near the bottom of the hill directly in front of me. Then I heard a muffled boom. A few seconds later it happened again, but this time a little closer. After the third one, I realized this was an enemy mortar attack.

When I saw that the mortars were getting closer to the front gate with every new round, I used my best military training and immediately panicked. After the frightful attack last night I wasn't going to take any chances. I called the sergeant of the guards and told him what I was witnessing.

He calmly said, "Don't worry. This happens every other morning and they never hit anything. Just stay at your post and they'll stop in a minute."

Like the sergeant said, the mortars stopped without hitting a thing. I didn't wet my pants this time, but I came close.

I continued my guard duty for two more days before I was shipped out to my permanent assignment. I had to salute officers every morning but there were no more mortar attacks, thank God. On my final day at Long Bien, the duty roster said I was to report to the company clerk at 1030 hours. I walked into the clerk's office. Without looking up he said, "What's yer name, private?"

I told him my name and he handed me a stack of papers. He instructed me to report to the airfield right away.

As I walked away, I read the papers. They said I was assigned to the Americal Division, C Company, 3rd Battalion of the 1st Infantry, 11th Light Infantry Brigade. I had no idea what that meant, but it sounded impressive.

After I picked up my gear from the barracks and was walking to the airfield it occurred to me I was getting closer to an actual combat mission. Instead of fear, pride swelled up in me. I was pumped up. I was riding an adrenaline high. I felt invincible. I was going out to "fight the enemy" and come back a hero. I was feeling the godlike power I would later feel again that comes from carrying a loaded weapon and having the ability to take a human life.

I walked with my chest out and my head held high. I was actually going to do a soldier's job! I was in a war! I was somebody! I belonged to a combat infantry unit, and I was damn proud to be a soldier in the United States Army!

An Army bus ferried me to Bien Hoa Air Base and dropped me near the briefing area where I had been when I first arrived in Vietnam a few nights ago. I was told I would take a cargo plane to Chu Lai and report to my division headquarters there.

Cargo planes are a common mode of transportation for soldiers, but I'd never been on a cargo plane before. In fact, I'd only been on a passenger airplane a couple of times in my life, including the trip here. Cargo planes are nothing like passenger planes; there are no seats. With no seats, there are no safety belts or anything to strap you in.

I stood at the edge of the runway waiting for the crew to finish loading the plane so I could board. After the cargo was stacked in, I was told to find a place to sit. I ended up sitting on top of the pallets of cargo with only a cargo net to hang on to. I was the only "live cargo" on this plane.

The rear door only covered about half the opening, so there was very little to prevent me from sliding off the stack of crates and right out the back of the plane.

During the ride, I got so scared, I puked. I thought about being so far away from home and in a place completely unknown to me, but that wasn't what frightened me. The thought of falling out of the damn cargo plane... now that frightened me!

When I arrived at Division Headquarters, I found my way to the clerk's office and checked in. The clerk was a chubby redhead with a toothy grin and a pleasant attitude. He informed me I was required to spend a week training in Chu Lai before being sent to the field. I spent another week learning about the Vietnamese culture, the Viet Cong, land mines and gas attacks.

I went through the booby trap course and managed to survive it without getting blown up. I found all the booby traps and disarmed every one of them. I was proud, I was smart and I was strong. I thought, "I'm a pretty darn good soldier."

Still, it all seemed like a game. Chu Lai was a very secure base camp and the training was controlled, so there were no injuries. The full impact of human warfare had not yet hit me and I still didn't have my own gun.

After completing the training period in Chu Lai, I was sent to a place called LZ (landing zone) Bronco. It was near the village of Duc Pho. Duc Pho was reported to be the birthplace of Ho Chi Minh, a revered political figure in South Vietnam. I had heard the name before but had no idea who he was or why he was so revered.

Anyway, LZ Bronco was the headquarters area for the 11th Light Infantry Brigade and was where I would be supplied to go out in the field. The big moment was coming. I was finally going to get my own rifle and ammunition.

I reported to the company clerk at C Company, 3rd Battalion of the 1st Infantry (also known as C 3/1). I was sure he was going to tell me I needed more training or a physical exam, but he surprised me by telling me I was to go directly to the supply tent and get outfitted to go to the field *today*.

I rushed to the supply tent where the supply sergeant told me I wouldn't need all that gear issued to me prior to leaving the states. He took all my nice, new uniforms and equipment and resupplied me with nice, *used* uniforms and equipment.

I hadn't thought much about the fact I would be carrying a week's supply of food, water, clothing and heavy ammunition on my back. The sergeant made it crystal clear there was no room in my pack for anything other than the bare necessities.

The supply sergeant, in all his kindness, issued me an army pack commonly called a "butt pounder," so called because it hung low on your back and had a tendency to pound you in the butt when you walked. The more full it got, the more pronounced the effect. He told me there was a shortage of the newer back packs (known as rucksacks) and as soon as one was available he'd send it out to me.

Yeah, right! I was beginning to see there were people in the Army, and especially here in Vietnam, who didn't have my best interests at heart. I later heard a rumor that some of the newer equipment was being sold on the black market.

Last, but not least, I was finally issued my very own, and quite well-used, M-16 rifle. The supply sergeant made a point to inform me that this rifle with its unique serial number, was issued to me personally. He told me I was responsible for its well being and if it got lost or damaged, I would be held personally liable and have to pay for the weapon before another would be issued.

This bothered me a little. I thought the Army would have enough rifles that if one was lost, stolen or damaged they would just replace it without question, especially since I needed it to do my job. The information took some of the thrill out of having my own weapon.

The supply sergeant sent me to the ammo bunker down by the helicopter pad to pick up ammunition and food. He told me to get at least enough food and ammo to last a week.

The ammo bunker looked like a big pile of neatly stacked sand bags with a door at one end. The supply clerk said I could have all the food and ammo I felt I could carry.

I was surprised at how heavy the C-rations were. C-rations were packaged, canned and dried food, most left over from previous wars. The supply clerk showed me how to attach a case of C-rations to the straps above my "butt pounder" and how to strap bandoliers of ammo on my hips.

When I put on all the gear and picked up my rifle, I was amazed at how heavy I felt. I was a young man, healthy and physically fit. Yet I was wondering, "How am I going to fight the enemy with all this heavy gear hanging on my body?" It seemed an impossibility to lug all these heavy supplies and equipment and still have the energy to fight the war.

The supply clerk must have read my thoughts because he looked at me and said, "Don't worry, you'll get used to it." He put his hand on my shoulder and pointed to the flat ground below the ammo bunker. He said, "Go wait there for your chopper. It'll be here in about ten minutes."

As I stood on the chopper pad waiting for a ride to my combat unit, I was thinking I was once again alone. It seemed ever since leaving basic training, I had been alone. There were always people with me, but no one I could call a friend.

When I was growing up I always had close pals, someone I could talk to or rely on to help with any problems. But now, I was truly alone. There was no one to turn to.

My youth and inexperience gave me false courage. Some of the fear of going to combat had subsided since the mortar attacks at Long Bien.

Now I had a gnawing in my gut and a feeling of apprehension telling me that I was entering into something very serious. I had just the tiniest insight into why the drill sergeants thought it was so foolish to volunteer to be an infantry soldier and go to Vietnam.

Chapter 5

Going to the Field

My heart rose to my throat when I heard the "thwap, thwap, thwaping" of the Huey helicopter arriving to carry me to meet my new unit. The sound of its approach was enough to send chills up my spine. As it landed, dust and dirt flew everywhere and it was hard to move forward against the windstorm of the rotor blade's thrust. It was impossible to hear over the roar of the turbine engine and the spinning of the blades.

The door gunner, with his M-60 machine gun dangling in front of him, waved me into the open cargo bay. There was a gunner on each side and no doors or seats in the cargo bay, just a big open space behind the pilots. This was my first time on a helicopter. Although I had seen them from a distance, I had no idea of the awesome power and emotion this mighty war machine could conjure.

I moved unsteadily toward the cargo bay of the Huey. The blast of air from the rotor blades made it difficult to walk. This was both exciting and frightening at the same time. I climbed on board and sat against the back wall of the cargo bay, facing the pilots.

The pilot in the left seat turned and gave me a little wave. Then the chopper began vibrating heavily as we lifted off the ground in a swirl of dust.

The flight was exhilarating and the view out the open doors was breathtaking. Vietnam was a beautiful country with rice paddies dotting the valley and gentle hills rising from the valley floor. The thrill of riding in this helicopter made me feel excited to be alive and on my way to my first real combat duty.

The Huey dropped me at a small outpost somewhere in the middle of the Quang Ngai province. They called it a "fire support base" and as far as I know it had no name. Many of the larger firebases, as they were sometimes called, were given names like Firebase Charlie or Firebase Maggie. Some of the firebases, like this one, were temporary and mobile so they could be set up and torn down quickly.

This particular firebase was on the top of a hill overlooking the valley. Two flat spots had been bulldozed on the hill, one for helicopters to land on and the other for artillery guns, mortars and a command tent. The perimeter of the firebase was dotted with fox holes, obviously dug by hand. A makeshift tent city was tucked on the backside of the hill. It housed the infantry soldiers, like myself, who were protecting the hill by night and running patrols into the valley by day.

I stood on the chopper pad wondering where I should go and where to report. A young man in a dirty uniform wearing no rank or unit insignias walked up to me and said, "You must be the new guy. Follow me. I'll take you to your area."

He led me to the tent city and informed me that my squad (about ten guys) was out on patrol, but they would be back in an hour or so.

I immediately noticed the tents weren't tents at all, but were actually Army issue ponchos staked out like tents over shallow holes. I ate one of my C-ration meals while I waited for my new squad to return. I was still feeling the high from my first chopper ride and hadn't had time to feel fear or concern about the enemy. Cognitively, I was aware I was now in the combat zone, but emotionally it hadn't hit me yet.

When the squad returned from patrol, I met the squad leader, Sergeant Russell, and a couple of the other guys from the squad. I was buddied-up with John, a young-looking, blond fellow from Detroit.

John had only arrived there a few days before I did but seemed to know the ropes already. I found out that in Vietnam you either learned quickly or quickly died. Later, I met some of the other soldiers in my unit and that night I pulled guard duty.

There were two men to a foxhole on guard duty and we were guarding the perimeter of the firebase. The man I was paired with was from a different squad but in the same platoon that I was in. He had been in Vietnam almost two months and he looked like a hardened veteran to me.

Guard duty required the use of a radio. In training we had never really used a radio much so I didn't know exactly what to say or how to say it. I knew that a phonetic alphabet was used to help clarify communication and that you had to say "over" when you finished talking.

Everyone else seemed fluent in radio lingo, rapidly quipping radio jive back and forth. It seemed that everyone knew the jargon, except me. I didn't feel scared on guard duty. I felt stupid.

By the end of my shift I was able to understand some of the terminology, but I had a long way to go before becoming fluent. I finished my two hours of guard duty, then crawled into my tent and went to sleep.

The next morning, I woke up and got out some C-rations for breakfast. John showed me how to make a stove out of a couple of used cans and how to use C-4 plastic explosive to heat the stove.

Burning plastic explosive in the stove seemed like risky business. John assured me it was safe as long as I used only a small amount and didn't try to step on it to put it out.

The C-4 burned very hot and fast–within a couple minutes my meal was piping hot. I was beginning to see there was a lot more to being in combat than was taught in training.

While we were eating breakfast, the squad leader came to tell us to be ready to go out on a short patrol at 0930 hours.

Until my arrival at this outpost, I'd always been at much larger base camps which were much more secured. The larger base camps had barbed wire fences, flood lights, tents and mess halls, all in fairly secure areas.

This place wasn't at all secure. There were no barbed wire fences in front of us, just foxholes. Foxholes lined the perimeter, and someone had to be on guard in those foxholes twenty-four hours a day. I hadn't noticed the previous day that these foxholes were manned. During the day there was only one man in every other hole. There was a good field of vision during daylight hours so the guards were much more casual than at night.

The First Patrol

At 0930 Sgt. Russell came by and said we would be leaving on a short patrol in a few minutes and that we would be "traveling light." John told me "traveling light" meant we only needed to take our rifle with an extra magazine of ammo and our canteens.

I strapped the necessary gear to my waist, put my steel helmet on and loaded my weapon. This was my first true realization I had a live weapon and that I was positioning myself to fire my weapon in combat. I was readying myself to do battle against a live human enemy. This was the first time I started to become deeply afraid of being in combat. I began to realize the enemy could be hiding anywhere and they could shoot from anywhere at anytime.

We moved beyond the perimeter of the little firebase, walking in a long line down an open trail. Suddenly, the fear gripped me. I was really scared. My mouth began to dry out and I began to sweat profusely.

When I couldn't sweat anymore, it felt like my body was on fire. I was extremely hot and couldn't cool down. I started to shake and felt like my head was coming apart. We had only been walking about ten minutes but every step was pure torture. I was surprised, and relieved, when the sergeant told us to take a short break.

I hid in the bushes away from everyone because I didn't want anyone to know how scared I was. I was hyperventilating and I had dry heaves. My heart pounded and I couldn't control my fear. I thought I was going to die of fright. Never in my life had I ever been so scared.

The sergeant motioned for the squad to reassemble and we walked back to the firebase. After drinking my entire canteen of water, I calmed down enough to walk back without showing the full extent of my fear.

When we got back, I ran to my little tent and hid. I shook uncontrollably. I thought, "My God! I have to endure a full year of this."

We had only gone about two hundred yards outside the perimeter. We were never out of visual contact with the firebase, and were only gone about twenty-five minutes. I couldn't imagine what it was going to be like to be out on patrol for days or weeks at a time.

John stuck his head in the tent to see how I was doing. He didn't say anything about my being scared, but I'm sure he knew. We talked about how silly the patrol had been. Then laughed about how much effort we all went through just so the sergeant could take a better look into the valley to gather information for his daily report.

As we were talking, I heard a chopper coming in to the landing pad. John said the chopper was probably bringing another new guy to join our squad today. That felt good; it meant I was no longer the newest guy on the team. I felt like I had just been promoted.

The new guy, Hank, was a tall, slim, New Yorker with a big grin and a strong handshake. He was eighteen years old, like John and I, although I suspected John had lied about his age to get into the Army and was probably closer to seventeen.

I wasn't really looking to make friends this quickly but the three of us bonded almost instantly. From the moment John and I met Hank, the three of us were inseparable.

The next day I learned we would be going out for a longer stint in the field, maybe a week or two. The sergeant informed us we would be on a company-wide operation and would possibly be choppering into a hot LZ (any place where a chopper would land was called an LZ, landing zone). A hot LZ meant that there was a good chance we would be taking incoming fire as the helicopters landed.

Sgt. Russell took the three new guys (John, Hank, and myself) aside. He explained that if the landing zone was hot the helicopters would not actually land. Under those circumstances they would come in low to the ground and we would have to get out very quickly. He also informed us we would have to lay down cover fire so the choppers could get out as fast as possible.

This was a very frightening scenario. I remembered how scared I was just walking outside the perimeter of this little firebase. I couldn't imagine how I would feel trying to hurry out of a hovering helicopter with all my gear strapped to my body while someone was shooting at me and trying to kill me. My stomach was in knots and I was sweating profusely but I didn't want the others to know how frightened I was. We were all very quiet and I imagined John and Hank were having similar feelings.

That evening we helped each other pack our gear and prepare for our first "combat assault." Guard duty seemed less demanding than previous nights and I was beginning to catch on to the radio jargon. Sharing these experiences with my new buddies made being in the war zone a little less intimidating.

We all assembled on the chopper pad early in the morning. I was really nervous, but I wasn't as scared as the day before. What worried me most was doing the wrong thing or screwing up and getting someone hurt. I wanted to be a good soldier and fit in like "one of the guys." I was impressed with the way the veterans calmly prepared for battle and seemed to know instinctively what to do.

I could hear the choppers coming in from the north. The sound of the rotor blades made my heart pound loudly in my ears. The sight of a dozen choppers coming across the hills was inspiring. It gave me a sense of power that I hadn't felt before. Suddenly my fear was replaced by a sense of pride, a sense of teamwork. Working together with a large group of men in a coordinated effort utilizing high tech, modern warfare equipment gave me a feeling of invincibility.

We were divided into groups of eight and instructed to get on our assigned chopper as soon as it landed. Our threesome was in the same group, along with Sgt. Russell. The sergeant told us to keep an eye on him. He would tell us when to get off the chopper and where to go once we were on the ground.

The helicopter flight was exhilarating. The adrenaline was pounding through my veins. I looked at the faces of the men around me and felt a sense of unity. This is what I trained for. I was now a real combat soldier just like John Wayne. I was fighting for my country and I was honored to be in the United States Army. I was fighting to prevent the spread of communism and making the world a better place to live.

A Strange Noise

The sergeant instructed us to jump from the helicopter, stay low and run for the cover of the trees. I was so nervous my legs felt like rubber.

When I jumped out of the helicopter, I landed in a wet, muddy, rice paddy. I tried to run, but my feet were stuck. As I freed them and began running, I heard a strange noise. "Splat, splat. Crack, crack."

It didn't take long to realize the noise was the sound of bullets landing all around me, splashing in the water. The crack-crack was the sound of the bullet breaking the sound barrier.

I couldn't see or hear the muzzle of the weapon that fired the bullets, only the crack-crack sound the bullet made afterward. It was such a foreign sound.

In training, I didn't remember the bullets making a cracking sound. It was an odd sound, much different than the sound made when firing the bullet away from you.

There's an old saying, "Ya' never hear the one that gets ya'." There's truth to that because you never hear the crack of the bullet until it passes by you.

It was in this rice paddy I began to understand this was no summer camping trip, accelerated Boy Scout adventure or game. This was serious and very dangerous. This was war. Even in my moments of shock and terror, I was in awe of the power of the war.

No one was injured in the helicopter assault. The enemy stopped firing as soon as the helicopters left. I was surprised I was able to overcome my fear. In fact, I was feeling pretty good about my first few moments of combat. As I proudly moved to where the rest of my unit was gathering, I looked down and felt a little sheepish as I realized I hadn't taken my weapon off safety.

We regrouped by the tree line and began moving down the little valley. I could see men moving ahead of me, but I was quite far back in the line and couldn't see the front.

Pretty soon I heard the crack-crack sound again. This time I could hear a lot of shooting going on, but no bullets were coming close to me. I hit the ground, rolled and found cover. Then I heard one of the guys up front call, "Medic," and I knew someone had been hit. What I didn't know was that someone had been killed.

The shooting stopped and a medevac helicopter came in to pick up the dead man. By the time I passed by where he had been, the body had been taken away. It was an uncomfortable feeling. Since I didn't actually see the body, I didn't really feel much. I remember thinking, "Well, I didn't even know him," and then I felt slightly guilty because deep inside I was relieved it was him and not me.

The Beginning of Acclimation

As the week went on, the days seemed to blur together. We moved along on our daily patrols of the valley. Our unit was shot at a couple more times, but nothing serious happened and no one was hurt. When we finished the operation we were choppered to LZ Liz, the firebase our company used as a base of operations when we were not in the field (some firebases were called LZs. I'm not sure what the difference was, if any).

LZ Liz was a firebase a few miles north of LZ Bronco. It was much bigger than the outpost we were on when I first went to the field. Liz was a base of operations for two companies of infantry, a mortar unit, an artillery battery and a communications unit. The perimeter had permanent bunkers made of sandbags, corrugated metal sheeting and wood planks. There were several supply and operations buildings within the perimeter. The infantry soldiers lived in the perimeter bunkers and took turns on guard duty twenty-four hours a day. We ran daily patrols around LZ Liz, although I was never sure what purpose it served.

I was starting to get to know some of the guys and I was starting to settle in to the war zone. I was adjusting to the humid climate, the heat and the hostile environment. It wasn't just the enemy that made the environment hostile. There were insects and snakes that could kill as easily as a man with a weapon.

On my second day at LZ Liz, I was standing near my bunker when I noticed a group of Vietnamese men carrying an old woman up the hill. I notified a couple of guys in my squad they were coming and we walked down the road to meet them.

The woman had been shot in the mouth and her face was badly torn up. It bothered me. I thought, "Who would shoot this old woman in the face?"

The men didn't speak English so we couldn't understand exactly what they were saying. I knew they wanted help, but I wasn't quite sure how to treat them. They weren't dressed as soldiers. They were just a few old men and an injured woman. We had learned in training that the Viet Cong often played on the sympathies of American soldiers and used women, children and the elderly to lure them into deadly traps.

We had been taught that they weren't real people, they were just gooks, the enemy. In training we were taught to think of the indigenous people and enemies as something less than human. The drill instructors had called them "gooks,"which I later found out was a Korean word meaning "man."

This scene was not congruent with the battles we had fought. This woman was a casualty of war, but was not necessarily a combatant. She wasn't dressed in soldier's fatigues, but indeed, to me, she was the enemy. It was an odd sensation. Seeing this dying woman, I wanted to be compassionate and do something to help her. On the other hand, I had to be very wary of a trap which could cost us our lives.

My buddies seemed cold and indifferent. They scoffed, "So what? She's an old woman, let her die."

They had no compassion and I could afford no compassion. It was too much risk to stay around her and too much risk to bring her onto the firebase. I couldn't see her as a person; she was the enemy.

In the end, we sent these people away without rendering any aid. In my heart, I was shocked at my behavior, I wanted to feel for her, but the risk was too great.

I was beginning to recognize there was a psychological and emotional struggle going on inside me. In my heart I was still an innocent young man, but in my head I was a highly trained, combat infantryman. I wasn't sure how to handle this battle between my heart and my head. My heart was heavy and yet my head was still able to justify my behavior.

Later that day Sgt. Russell stuck his head in the bunker where John, Hank and I were on guard. He said, "I found some gear down by the chopper pad and thought you new guys might be able to use it."

When we looked up at him, he tossed three brand new rucksacks into the bunker. We were ecstatic. This was our initiation into the ranks of the veterans and indicated we had proved ourselves as worthy soldiers in combat. This was Sgt. Russell's way of rewarding us for a job well done.

Within A Heartbeat

The next day I went out on patrol with a small group that included John and Hank. I felt better about being on patrol, but I was a little nervous because I didn't know the area. Since the newer guys weren't experienced enough yet, we were not asked to walk point. I was in the middle of the pack, walking behind John.

We were walking along a trail in what was thought to be a fairly secure area and I was laughing and joking with John. We weren't talking loudly but since we were out in the open and could easily be seen, there was no need to be perfectly quiet. Inside I was still scared, but I had learned to put on this false bravado so no one would know how scared I was.

Within a heartbeat, I heard crack-crack, crack-crack. Just two shots passing me and that was it. Everybody got down and waited. It was suddenly very quiet. All I could hear was the pounding of my own heart.

Suddenly someone yelled, "Medic!"

This time I wasn't far from the front and I saw my first dead G.I. It was Sgt. Russell. I realized I barely knew him. I stared at him lying on the ground in an awkward position. There wasn't a lot of blood, but he was dead. He still looked the same, but the life had gone out of him. It was so strange. I wasn't shocked at what I saw, but I had an empty feeling in the pit of my stomach.

I thought, "I should feel something. I should feel bad; I've never seen a dead person before." It was surreal. He had just been walking along with the rest of us, on a routine patrol, and now, he was dead in a heartbeat.

I didn't understand my reaction. As I stood there looking at Sgt. Russell, death didn't seem so terrible. Then for just a brief moment, I thought, "I'm glad it was you and not me."

We called in a chopper and a couple of guys bagged him up, loaded him on and sent him off. We continued with our patrol, business as usual. Nobody said anything.

The next day the chaplain came and we had a memorial service for the sergeant. It seemed like a generic service with the sergeant's name inserted at the appropriate place in the text. But what did I know about funeral services? I'd never ever been to one. I'd never even thought very deeply about death. Sure it happened...to other people.

Pretty soon, our unit was going on more and more patrols, deeper into the field and into more intense firefights. We were often picked up and taken by helicopter to hot LZs. I learned that we were now part of a reactionary force that would respond when there were other units in trouble. We would also be sent where there was suspected enemy movement. It was our job to engage the enemy wherever and whenever our commanders felt the need.

John, Hank and I were forming a strong brotherhood. We fought side-by-side, always providing covering fire for each other. We vowed to always be there to keep each other safe. We ate together, pulled guard duty together and went on patrols and missions together as a team as often as possible.

We had a saying, "In death or just fun, these three are but one." We worked so well together it was almost as if we could read each other's minds.

Hardening to War

On every patrol now several men died and another four or five were wounded. We'd experienced many intense battles, and had been hit hard on several occasions. After less than ten weeks, I had seen dozens of dead and wounded bodies on both sides of the fighting. In the wake of a firefight, there were often many dead Vietnamese bodies to be counted and searched. Days and events began to grow fuzzy. I started losing track of time. My head was beginning to overrule my heart. I was now an experienced combat veteran.

I had quickly become a hardened soldier, willing to do whatever it took to stay alive and accomplish my mission. I felt less and less discomfort about the death, pain and anguish that accompanied every firefight. I was becoming increasingly focused on my own survival.

The Insanity of War

Although I was becoming more accustomed to the brutality of war, I still had a lot of emotion bottled up inside. Our company commander had finished his tour of duty and had gone home. He was well-liked by the men and was a very intelligent leader. The new commander was a captain with a West Point education and an exaggerated sense of self-importance. He came to our company on the eve of a big operation. It was an operation that would take us on a sweep through the Quang Ngai Valley and up into the hills near the border of Laos.

We had only been out in the field a few days before it became clear that this new commander wasn't anywhere near as astute at soldiering as our previous commander had been. We had marched at a fairly rapid pace and were ahead of schedule. The commander decided to set up a perimeter in the early afternoon and do some search and destroy missions in the abandoned villages nearby.

Our squad had been digging a series of foxholes on the south side of the perimeter when the commander called and asked for some volunteers. He wanted a small squad of men to go to the abandoned village in front of our position and search for any signs of enemy activity.

Ron, our new squad leader, was a nice guy who got along well with everyone. He rarely ever delegated dangerous duty without volunteering to go himself. This day was no exception. Ron asked Hank, myself and few of the others if we would go with him to the village and take a look around. This seemed like a pretty routine patrol.

The village consisted of six or seven straw and bamboo huts built on clay foundations. When we got there, we found no signs of life. We carefully checked all the huts and looked for hidden doorways or tunnels. When we were convinced that this area had been thoroughly searched and was clear of any potential danger, we rallied in the middle of the village.

By consensus we agreed that the village had been abandoned the day before when we had called in artillery to soften the area before our arrival. We decided to take one more look around the outside of the village before returning to our encampment.

We searched along the edge of the village and came upon an unusual sight. There was a dead Vietnamese woman lying flat on her back with an agonized look plastered on her face. Directly between her outstretched feet was an unexploded artillery round. The projectile was half buried in the dirt and must have landed during the previous day's shelling.

It appeared to us that the woman was going down the path to escape the village when the dud round landed at her feet. She must have died instantly of a heart attack when the round landed, because there was no blood or indication of physical injury.

Since she did not appear to be a soldier, we left her body where we found it so her people could identify her and bury her properly. We made our way back to the camp and radioed our report to the company commander, including the discovery of the dead woman.

He was quite upset that we hadn't buried this poor woman. Even after we explained it wouldn't be proper for us to bury her, he ordered us to return to the site and bury her.

We were upset with the commander's insensitive order because we always tried to follow certain ethics regarding the indigenous people. They all had different rituals. We knew any attempt to disturb this poor dead woman would be viewed, in their culture, as an act of disrespect. Regardless of our concerns, we had to follow orders and go back to bury the dead woman.

Ron, Hank, myself and one other man from our squad volunteered to go back to do the job. We left our heavy steel helmets and bulky packs in camp and walked back to the village.

We had no sooner started digging the grave when I looked up and saw an air-support spotter plane circling our position.

At first, I thought he had spotted some enemy soldiers in the area and was going to provide some protective fire for us. Then I realized that from the air we probably looked a lot like

North Vietnamese regulars. Immediately I thought, "Shit! That stupid commander didn't notify air-support he sent us out here."

I grabbed Ron by the arm and when he looked at me I knew he was thinking the same thing. Before we could start back to camp, the spotter dropped a smoke grenade on our position to mark it for the fighter jets.

Hank and the other guy started running for the perimeter of our camp. Ron had left his rifle leaning against a small tree and went back to get it, so I waited for him. Hank and the other guy were halfway to the perimeter by the time Ron and I started running into the dry rice paddies.

I could hear the fighter jets bearing down on us and when I looked up they had already released their napalm canisters. I motioned for Ron to hit the ground, hoping beyond hope that we would survive the attack. The searing heat from the napalm sucked our breath away, but fortunately the canisters landed fifty feet or so from our position. The inferno of deadly jelly splashed away from us.

I knew the jets would try to make another run on us. This time I was sure they would use their high-explosive bombs instead of napalm.

As quickly as I could, I got up and ran for the perimeter. I wasn't sure I could make it all the way before the jets circled and made another attack on us.

About forty feet in front of us, I spotted a rice paddy dike. It was about a foot high, two feet wide and ran the length of the paddy. The dike looked like it might afford some cover when they dropped the bombs. I looked back to check on Ron and saw he was on his knees. He had sprained his ankle in one of the ruts in the paddy.

I ran back to him and helped him to his feet. Then I told him we had to make it to the dike before the jets dropped their next load.

We started running, but Ron had a pronounced limp. When I tried to help him, he said, "Run as fast as you can. I can keep up with you."

I heard the scream of the jet engines. When I looked up, the bombs were already on the way down. As I leaped over the rice paddy dike, I peered back and saw Ron only about ten feet behind me. I was sure he would make it before the bombs landed so I tucked my head down and waited for the blast.

The explosion was loud and I could hear large pieces of shrapnel and debris whizzing over my head. The concussion of the blast tore my shirt and broke my M16 rifle in half. I was bleeding from the mouth and nose and temporarily deafened by the ringing in my ears.

As I looked up, I could see a large piece of metal from the bomb casing had penetrated the dike. The metal was only inches from my head. It took a minute or two after the blast cleared to inventory myself and determine that I was still in one piece.

I stood up and looked behind me for Ron. He wasn't there. I didn't want to look toward the bomb crater, but I had to.

There on the edge of the crater were the remains of my friend, Ron. The bombs had shredded his body. The meat was torn from his bones and his guts were spilled out on the ground.

I heard a slight moan from him and I ran to get the medics, knowing that there was no hope. But I had to try.

Hank must have gotten to a radio and called off the air strike because the jets did not make another pass.

As I approached the perimeter, the medics were already on their way. I turned and followed them back to where Ron's lifeless body was lying. They gave it their best efforts, but there was nothing the medics could do to save him.

Tears welled up in my eyes. I sobbed uncontrollably. Ron was my friend and a truly nice person. The emotions I had bottled up inside me came pouring out. I hurt more deeply than I ever hurt before in my life. My entire body and soul ached.

As the medevac chopper left with the remains of my comrade, I walked slowly back to the perimeter. My distress over the loss of my friend turned to rage. That moron of a company commander had sent us on a ridiculous mission and he had failed to notify air-support we were out there. I was seeing red. I knew I had to kill that son-of-a-bitch before anyone else was hurt by his incompetence.

John and Hank met me when I entered the camp. I was near insane with anger and kept repeating, "I'm going to kill that bastard. I'm going to kill the fucking company commander and no one is going to stop me."

John and Hank, being the good friends they were, knew I was dead serious. They weren't about to let me proceed. They got a couple other guys to help tie me up and throw me in a hole. Hank said, "You're gonna stay there until you calm down and agree that you won't do anything stupid." Then he crouched down close to me and said, "Everybody in the company knows what happened and we will handle the situation so we'll all be safe. Now shut up and calm down."

It took a couple of hours before I was calm enough for them to untie me and let me loose. Even though they trusted me, John and Hank kept an eye on me all night and pulled my guard duty for me. They knew how deeply hurt I was over Ron's senseless death.

Ron's death did something to me. It changed the way I perceived the war effort. It destroyed my faith that the Army would provide leadership and keep us safe. From that point on, I believed I could not trust our leaders and that I would have to make decisions based on my own judgment of a situation. I knew I could trust John and Hank, but that was as far as my trust could go.

As we continued on our mission, the commander led us further into the valley. We were expecting to meet heavy resistance in the next few days and we were all on edge.

While patrolling, we stopped for a lunch break in an area that was slightly wooded and had some hedgerows separating the villages and rice paddies. Hank and I told the platoon leader we were going to move down the trail about fifty yards and set up a rear guard while we ate lunch.

Hank and I really just wanted to get away from the rest of the group and relax. We found a shady spot under a tree where we were somewhat hidden but had a clear field of vision.

We were eating our lunch and quietly talking when I saw a man dressed in the typical "black pajama" outfit of the rural Vietnamese people and most of the Viet Cong soldiers. The Viet Cong were guerilla fighters who sympathized with the North Vietnamese regime. The man was walking toward us on a small path that ran alongside a thick hedgerow. Our platoon was eating lunch just beyond the hedgerow and I was concerned that this Vietnamese man might have a weapon or an explosive device hidden in the hedge.

I watched him for a few minutes as he walked slowly and kept looking in the hedge, but I couldn't tell exactly what he was doing or looking for. Hank and I were facing in opposite directions so he didn't see the man and I said nothing to him as I watched.

As the man got closer to our position I carefully picked up my weapon. I still hadn't said a word to Hank as he quietly ate his lunch.

I put the rifle to my shoulder and had the man's chest in my sights. Hank started to say something. I quickly motioned for him not to speak.

I assumed that the man was Viet Cong and had weapons hidden in the hedge. The Viet Cong often came disguised as grandfathers, children and women pedaling wares and carrying infants. They were civilians by day, soldiers by night.

Unlike the North Vietnamese Army (NVA), a well-trained and well-equipped fighting force, the Viet Cong were an underground resistance army, well versed in guerrilla tactics. This made it difficult to know who the enemy was or where they would be hiding. It was one of the most demoralizing psychological effects of this war.

The man was now thirty feet from where we were sitting and Hank turned his head to look. The Vietnamese man stopped and was standing there as if he sensed the danger. Before he could turn and run, I calmly pulled the trigger.

As the man fell to the ground, I pulled the trigger four more times. By the time his body was lying prone on the ground, he was dead.

My first reaction was elation. This was my first direct kill. Although I had been in many firefights, it was rare to know exactly whom you hit or if you hit anyone at all. Having a confirmed kill was a big deal for an infantryman.

Hank reached over and patted me on the back and said, "Way to go, pal."

Several of the guys from our platoon came over to find out what the shooting was about. They shook my hand and congratulated me on the kill. By the time I walked over to see the body, I was feeling uncomfortable. I wasn't sure that this was such a good thing I had done.

When I looked at the body of this Vietnamese man lying on the ground, dead from the wounds I had inflicted, I ran to the bushes and puked my guts out. I couldn't understand why everyone thought the killing was so special. It wasn't special. It was horrible and it was ugly.

I felt ashamed of myself for what I had done. Internally, I was battling a moral dilemma. The Army said it was all right to kill, but morally I knew it was wrong.

The platoon leader said if this man had detonated an explosive device in the midst of our lunch group, a lot of men would have died. He said I saved lives by killing this man. I didn't feel like a hero, I felt evil. I thought about this man's family and friends and how much they would miss him. I wondered if he was married and had children.

I had to ignore my emotions because the feelings of guilt, shame and horror at my acts were not feelings I could share with the other men. Not even John and Hank were privy to my deepest inner feelings. It was just too much to cope with. I couldn't afford the time to process or feel my emotions with all the pressure of fighting this war.

Another Dead Leader

The following day the company split up into three groups to sweep through the hills and try to find where the enemy troops were hiding. The plan was that each group would go in a different direction. In a couple of days we would all come together again on the other side of the hills.

The incompetent commander was leading one group and a couple of the senior platoon leaders were in charge of the other two groups. The group I was in was assigned to move over to the left side of the hill and through a pass. It was rumored that the pass was used by the North Vietnamese Army to move supplies into the valley.

On the second day of the sweep we hadn't found any evidence that NVA troops had been anywhere in the area. We decided to start moving toward the rendezvous point so we could get there early the next morning. The platoon leader thought we needed some time to rest since the company commander had been driving us hard. He said if we got to the rendezvous point before the others, we could have a longer break.

This sounded like a great idea and we decided to push a little farther than normal. We wanted to be as close to the rendezvous point as possible before we made camp for the night.

As we moved out, I was at the rear of the column. I heard some commotion near the platoon leader. I walked ahead so I could see him. He was talking frantically on the radio, motioning us to move to the side of the trail and take a break.

The word came back that the headquarters group led by our blundering commander had been ambushed and there were several casualties. We were all concerned because we knew many of the guys in that group. We were helpless. They were a half-day march away from us. All we could do was pray the casualties were minimal.

That night we made camp and the platoon leader called a few of us over for a brief meeting. He said the casualties at the ambush were light, a few wounded and one KIA (killed in action).

The KIA was the company commander. He had ordered his squad to charge the ambush and when he stepped out to lead the charge, he was shot multiple times. The official report stated he was killed by hostile fire.

I didn't feel a thing when I heard the commander was dead. I had only one thought, "I'm glad he's gone. He's done enough damage to good men."

I tucked my thoughts back in the corner of my mind and returned to my duties. The next day we were ordered to return to LZ Liz.

Bell "Huey" helicopter used to transport troops and supplies to the field.

Hughes Helicopter - a Loach primarily used for reconnaissance.

Warrior Country at LZ Bronco, 11th Light Infantry Battalion Headquarters, Duc Pho.

LZ Liz Company Headquarters,
a firebase near the town of Duc Pho.

Welcome to LZ Liz! Entrance to LZ Liz. Lines are
for a helicopter landing pad.

Taking a break in the jungle.

Soldiers crossing a river after a firefight.

The men of Charlie Company getting fresh water from a stream as they move through the jungle.

Visiting a hootch in a friendly village.

In front of a hootch in a friendly village.

*One of the men from Charlie Company taking a
break in the jungle.*

Bill in the field early one morning.

*Bill at a firebase, leaning against a bunker,
drinking a beer.*

*Bill and the Medic sitting on sand bags
in front of a bunker.*

Some of the men of Charlie Company.

Chapter 6

Ambush

We ran regular patrols off LZ Liz and occasionally were sent for several days at a time to help other units that were engaging the enemy. The assignments, like time, blurred together until one particular incident awakened me to the subtle changes taking place in my personality.

We joined the rest of our company, along with our new company commander, on a mission into an area reported to contain several enemy strongholds. The new company commander was a decent man, not very experienced, but smart enough to take advice from the veteran officers and noncommissioned officers who had been in-country.

We were sweeping a village because there had been shots fired from that area. Suddenly, we were surrounded by an ambush. We were pinned down with nowhere to go.

Each time we tried to retreat from the village and regroup, we were met with heavy resistance. With each strategic move we tried, another man was wounded or killed. Each time we tried to retrieve our dead and wounded, the snipers picked off another of our men.

There were at least three dead and three wounded, and the wounded were screaming for help.

The ambush was very elaborate and very calculated. The enemy was well positioned and impossible to see. I was really scared, more than I had been in a very long time. They had us surrounded with no way out. They knew we wouldn't retreat and leave our wounded and dead behind (another of the codes we lived by).

The enemy shot to fatally wound rather than kill outright, to insure that the men died slowly and in great agony. The snipers held us at bay, rendering us helpless to rescue our friends and comrades. All we could do was find a safe place to hide from the enemy and listen to the sounds of suffering, torment and death.

There was nothing more demoralizing to me than to hear screams of terror and desperate pleas of men begging to be helped and not to be left behind. Mentally, the enemy was executing all of us!

While we were pinned down, helplessly listening to their screams, all the wounded died and the enemy fled.

We cautiously moved in and dragged the bodies out. We wrapped them in our plastic ponchos and tried to dig in for the night, knowing the enemy had not gone far. Each time we attempted to set up a protective perimeter for the night, we were fired on.

I was terrified and I was exhausted from carrying dead bodies. There were eight bodies and we had no desire to create more. Several of our leaders were dead. Our squad leader died along with our platoon sergeant and our medic was also killed.

With our squad leader dead, I was next in command to lead the squad. I had been in combat less than five months and now I was the senior ranking man in my squad. "Unbelievable!" I thought. I had celebrated my nineteenth birthday only a few weeks earlier, but I felt like a much older man. The situation seemed impossible.

As the sun began to set we knew we needed to come up with a plan to get out before darkness made us easy targets for the enemy. Those of us squad leaders that were left in command gathered around the company commander. A plan was decided.

We would pretend we were digging in for the night and just before dark, we would make a run for it. The commander said he would call for an artillery strike followed by an air strike, all of which would come in nearly on top of us as we ran from the village. He said he would try to get a couple of platoons in to provide covering fire while we ran out of the hot village.

We executed the plan perfectly. There were a few shots fired, but no one was injured. We carried our dead wrapped in ponchos and several men shouldered the burden for each body. The artillery came dangerously close. I could feel the concussion of the rounds exploding behind us as we ran.

As we cleared the village, I saw friendlies moving toward us to provide cover. It was dark as we set up a perimeter about a half-mile from the village and watched the air show.

During the ambush we had dropped our heavy backpacks so we could move more quickly. This is typical in combat. Usually, after the fighting ceased, we would return and retrieve our packs. This time we couldn't get back to where our gear was until the next day.

When I went to retrieve my pack, it was gone. The enemy had taken my backpack. With it, they stole a part of me. My address book, my pictures from home, half-written letters and all of my personal belongings were gone.

All the things that had any real meaning to me were now missing from my life. Those small things had helped me to remember who I was, where I came from and where I wanted to return. The enemy had taken my only connection to the real world, to the sanity of home.

I felt violated and angry. Worst of all, I felt empty! I stood there and could not believe my personal belongings were missing.

I wanted to do something to make this right, but there was absolutely nothing I could do.

A Matter of Survival

After that ambush, I realized that this war was insane. The only goal I could have was to return home, one way or another. It wasn't a matter of skill, technique, good maneuvers or good soldiering. It wasn't about a mission or a cause and it wasn't about developing good strategies. It wasn't even about winning the battle or winning the war. It was purely a matter of survival and that was all...just survival. If I survived for the duration of my tour, I would be able to go home and resume my life.

I began to understand that survival had to be my main focus and concern. If I were to remain alive, I had to eliminate everything that threatened to interfere with the goal of daily physical survival. I also realized that I had to work equally hard at psychological survival.

My personal thoughts and my personal feelings no longer had a place. Thoughts and feelings were a dangerous commodity. Valid or not, feelings had to go. They would interfere with my reactions and instincts. In an effort to survive, regard for others had to be extinguished.

I had to hone my instinct to survive in combat, remain constantly tuned and alert to my surroundings and deny all other internal activity. I had to learn to live by instinct alone. Reduced to the level of an animal, I no longer cared about anyone or anything other than my own personal survival.

After a while, I started to understand that survival was not just about living, but also about dying. Survival meant getting out of the war either alive as a whole human being or in a body bag. I cared nothing for myself, other than to hope for a quick death if it was my time to die.

I stopped ducking down during firefights. I stood up and fought back. Instinct taught me that there was no in-between. I had to kill or be killed. I had surrendered large chunks of myself, my personality had been altered and the transformation to a primitive state was complete. The war had won the battle for humanity. I was no longer fully human.

No Longer Human

I felt like a hunted and tormented animal. I became consumed with thoughts of killing, of taking human life and of striking back. I wanted to be the hunter, not the hunted. I wanted to inflict as much pain and agony on the enemy as possible and I wanted to keep the enemy as far away from me as I could. I believed and knew that there were only two ways out of this situation – death or the passage of time. I worked hard to achieve numbness. I didn't care about anything except protecting myself and staying alive, or dying. Either one was an adequate alternative.

Our squad had been under a lot of stress and I'd seen a lot of dying and death. As the months passed by, I became more accustomed to reacting in the basic survival "animal" mode. Sometimes I remembered that the Vietnamese were real people with families and friends. But those thoughts tortured me psychologically. I knew that I couldn't care and remain sane. "Animals don't care about their victims," I told myself, "so I don't care." I just wanted to stay alive, get back to my family and friends or die trying.

I realized that I was in a situation with only two options - life or death. There was nothing in between. This war had no rules, no guidelines and no reprieve. The psychological toll was mounting and the grinding realization set in. The longer I stayed in this "survivalist" state, the harder it would be and the longer it would take for me to come out of it. On some level, I knew there would never be a return to normalcy.

I was an animal and believed I had become an evil soldier. I remember the feeling well. Although I was not yet old enough to vote, to drink, or get married, I was deemed old enough to kill and die for my country. I was deemed old enough to experience man's grossest inhumanity against man. I was no longer human and judged myself to be evil because I had chosen to allow my animal instincts to be in control.

The Hardened Soldier

After nine months in combat, I'd seen an unconscionable amount of death, dying and maiming. I was numb inside. There was no more fear or worry left in me. I was a hardened combat soldier.

I was so apathetic that when we would get into firefights, everybody else would get down on the ground, but I would just stand up and watch. I'd just stand there and wait to see what direction the fire had come from. Then I would go and tell my soldiers where to shoot. The bullets would be whizzing right past me, rockets would be going off all around me, but I was numb to all of it. I wasn't heroic. I was simply devoid of all feeling. I would either conquer the enemy or die in the attempt.

I would calmly walk up and down the line telling my men where to shoot. I would be kicking, pointing and hollering at them, telling them to concentrate the fire over in one area or another. I wasn't even concerned about being shot. Instead, I was concerned with making sure we got to the enemy, over-powered the enemy, destroyed the enemy and drove them out of the area. Above all, I was concerned with making sure the enemy did not intimidate us.

As the numbness progressed, I realized I was actually no longer frightened. I was deadened inside and I just didn't care anymore. I thought, "Go ahead, shoot me. There are lots more where I came from. There's a whole bunch of us GIs here and we're all the same. We're all just a bunch of emotionally dead combat soldiers, ready to kill anything or anyone that stands in the way of returning home."

In the field, there is nothing that distinguishes one combat soldier from another except the skill to survive.

Good Buddies Make a Difference

John, Hank and I continued to grow closer. If there was any feeling left in me, it was the sense of kinship I felt for these two men. We had all become very good fighting men and were sometimes split apart to work with other squads or to lead small groups into combat situations. But we still remained close emotionally. We maintained our vow that as long as we stayed close, we would not let any harm come to one another.

In late January 1969, the three of us were recruited by the company commander to operate as a recon (reconnaissance) team. From time to time we would go on these recon missions independent of the main company.

When there were special missions, the three of us would go out in the jungle for three or four days at a time. We would gather information about enemy troop movements. Sometimes we would intervene, depending on the specifics of our mission. At times, our mission would be to monitor and plot enemy troop movements. At other times, we would be instructed to disrupt enemy troop movements by firing rockets at them or calling in artillery and air strikes. These recon missions were conducted along the Ho Chi Minh Trail where it entered Vietnam from Laos. We weren't supposed to be in Laos, but I'll bet we crossed the invisible line more than once.

John, Hank and I were so mentally attuned to one another that we rarely had to speak when we were in a difficult situation. We could almost anticipate each other's every move. These recon missions brought us closer together. While we were operating as a team, there was a sense of brotherhood I had never felt before with any man.

Our deep-seated trust for one another allowed us to drop our guard a little when we were away from the main unit. There was just enough of the child left in us that we were able to briefly laugh and play when it was safe to do so. This was the madness of the war. Under one set of circumstances I could skillfully manage the pressure of adult responsibility. In another situation I could feel the lightness of childhood. Nothing in this war made any sense.

The three of us agreed we were going to extend our tour of duty for another year. If we extended in six-month intervals, the Army would give us a month leave for every six-month tour. We figured we could take the first month at the end of our current tour and go home to see our families and friends.

We planned to take the second leave at the end of our first six-month tour and go traveling around Europe. We talked endlessly about it and dreamed of the day when we could make it all happen.

We always said that as long as the three of us were together to "cover" each other, nothing bad would happen and that way we believed we could eventually fulfill our dreams. My relationship with John and Hank was my only link to sanity. Without them, I certainly would have slipped even more deeply into my animalistic, survival mode.

The Fire of Fear

In April of 1969, with less than ninety days left to serve in Vietnam, I began the count down to the end of my tour. My thoughts were focused on returning home.

As soon as I started thinking about going home, I started having strange sensations. Emotions came flooding in. I was terrified I would not return home the same person I was when I left. I had already become someone I no longer recognized. I became completely enveloped by the fear. Everything that happened around me terrified me.

I hadn't felt anything at all for months and months and least of all, fear. And now, I was overwhelmed by it.

I was fearful about staying in Vietnam, but I was also extremely fearful about leaving Vietnam. I was a hardened combat soldier. While my friends were at home taking their dates to the movies and sipping root beer floats at the malt shop, I was killing the enemy.

At the age of nineteen, I had the power to take a human life and I exercised that power with a vengeance. To my friends back home, power was borrowing dad's car to go out partying on Friday night. I was a forty-year-old man in a nineteen-year-old body. My friends here in Vietnam could understand me. But I knew my friends back home would never understand what I had experienced in just one short year in the Vietnam War.

On April 16th, John and Hank received orders to take R&R (a rest and relaxation period usually spent in a neighboring country). I had taken mine in January. My R&R took me to Japan for a week where I tried to behave like a normal person in a surreal situation. I went from the steamy jungles of Vietnam to freezing snowy weather in Japan. It snowed almost the entire time I was there. While others went out on the town and slept with prostitutes, I stayed in my room, sweating and anxious.

Once, a prostitute came to my room soliciting, but she looked too much like the people I was killing in Vietnam and I sent her away. I went out to a bar a couple times, but the fear of being in a public place drove me back to my room. I hoped John and Hank would have a better time on R&R than I did. They didn't seem to be as affected by the war as I was, but then, we all pretended to be normal to each other.

I'll never forget the day the helicopter came and picked up John and Hank. They were gone, and I was left alone. I felt vulnerable without them.

Our squad was heading back to the base camp. I was in charge of a squad, which gave me something to do, but it was hard to return to the company without my buddies. We had been through so much together and we were all supposed to go home together. Yet they were gone on R & R, leaving me alone to face the enemy. My only consolation was we were just a day away from base camp and were not expecting any combat action.

In addition to my aloneness, I was uncomfortable with one particular guy in our unit. He was a real irritation to me— Tommy! He had only been with our unit a few months. But from the very first day, Tommy rubbed me the wrong way.

I gave commands, but in the clutch of the moment, Tommy choked. Tommy showed fear and I despised his fearfulness. As a result, we didn't get along well. I didn't like him and he didn't like me. But he was a member of my squad and I felt the need to be a good role model.

I had no way of knowing that Tommy would eventually play an enormous role in the changes that were about to take place in my life.

A Soldier's Eyes and Ears

John and Hank were gone and I did my best to maintain my composure while we marched back to the base camp. Our company was about 150 yards from the gate of the base camp when we got a call on the radio that a helicopter had been shot down. They requested four or five squads and a commander volunteer to go and find the downed chopper. We had to destroy the equipment and rescue the crew.

I volunteered my squad and thought, with the exception of Tommy, we were a very competent team. They needed competent, experienced squads to go in and get the job done and we had successfully done this type of job dozens of times before. I was good at it, my men were good at it and we all worked well together.

Several helicopters were sent in to pick us up and fly us over to the area near where the fallen chopper had been shot down. Although I didn't see the downed chopper when we flew over, I had an idea it was near the base of the hill. We landed on the south side of the hill where we suspected the downed chopper was located.

When I got off the helicopter, I thought, "Something's wrong. Something's really wrong!" I couldn't quite put my finger on it, but my animal instincts were telling me to beware.

We had been taking fire from several directions from the moment we got off the chopper, but that wasn't what was bothering me. I put my concerns aside as I moved away from the chopper and walked ahead. I needed to see where the fire was coming from so that I could move my men into position.

The men followed me, assured that I would not lead them into an ambush.

As my men positioned themselves on the ground, I stood up to see where the gunfire was coming from. I didn't have a radioman with my squad so the commander motioned to me to take my squad to the base of the hill and move north. In the meantime, his squad would move around the outside and flank us to the left.

Once again I sensed something was terribly wrong. I had a real uneasy feeling, an odd feeling I had never felt before during an assault. It seemed as though something unexpected was about to happen. I put on my best soldier ears and eyes and started moving through the bushes.

I led my squad through the bushes and rice paddies and started skirting the hill. Again we took fire from all sides.

I instructed my men to move to a safer area just ahead. This left me in a more open, unprotected area where I could better observe what was happening around me. I watched to see where the fire was coming from and then I fired my weapon right at the enemy's position.

I used a magazine that was loaded with tracer bullets so my squad could see the bullet pattern and know where to aim their fire. High hedgerows surrounded the rice paddies making it hard to see exactly where the enemy was and how many positions they had.

Friendly Fire

In a few minutes the gunshots started coming at us from all directions. It was heavier than ever. I knew it was more than just Viet Cong snipers or an NVA squad; it seemed more like a full NVA Company.

When we really started taking heavy fire, I got down in a shallow trench. As I got down, I looked up and saw two jet planes flying overhead. At that moment, I realized our commander must have been receiving as much fire as we were and called for an air strike. I instinctively knew the other squads must have been pinned down, too.

I watched the planes drop their bombs near the top of the hill. The first time they struck I thought, "Shit! If they drop those bombs too low on the hill, the shrapnel will blow back down on us. My God! If they drop those bombs too soon, they could land right on top of us."

The planes came over. I watched as they dropped the next load of bombs into the sky. I immediately knew they had released the bombs too early. I knew the bombs were going to land very close to my position. My men were safe because they were down low in the hedges along the rice paddy dike ahead of me. However, I was lying in not much more than a dip in the ground.

I knew there was no escape and no shelter for me. I got down as low as I could, closed my eyes and calmly waited for the bombs to hit.

Just before the bombs landed, I took a quick peek to see how close they were going to hit. I saw the bright flash, but before I could get my head back down, a big piece of red-hot shrapnel hit me in the face. The searing pain jolted my head back and my steel helmet tumbled to the ground. Smaller pieces of razor-sharp shrapnel hit me in the neck and down the right side of my body. I immediately realized I was badly hurt. The right side of my face was crushed by the baseball-sized piece of shrapnel from the bomb. The blood gushed from the wound and pooled beneath me in the dirt.

I leaned forward to pick up my steel helmet and, to my horror, I watched what was left of my right eye fall out into the helmet. My shirt was completely soaked with blood as it poured from the gaping holes in my body. I thought, "This is the end of the line for me. There is no medic here to rescue me and no radio to call for help. I'm dead... I'm gonna die right here...nineteen years old...thousands of miles from home."

All the things I'd never experienced in my short life rushed through my head. I'd never been in love. I'd never even had a real relationship with a woman. I had not really had a life, or at least the kind of life I'd always thought I might have. I wanted to be married and have a family. I wanted to kiss the kids and pet the dog on my way out to work every morning. I wanted to mow the lawn on sunny Saturday afternoons. I wanted to drink a cold beer while I barbequed for family and friends in the back yard of my own little house.

While I was lying on the ground, bleeding profusely, visions of the American Dream streamed through my head. Then, suddenly, it all came to a screaming halt. I was lying in the dust and dirt of a dry rice paddy in the Republic of Vietnam. I could see waves of heat rising from the hard ground. My men were safe on the other side of the rice paddy, and had no idea I was badly injured. The enemy was still firing at us from the hedgerows. I didn't care about any of this. All I could think was, "I'm going to die alone, no mom here to kiss it and make it better. I'm gonna die, right here, right now!"

Chapter 7

Bathed in The Light

Once I had accepted death and realized there was nothing else I could do, all the worry, fear and pain faded away. All that was left to do was relax and let it happen.

I took off my backpack, lay on the ground and made myself as comfortable as possible. I pulled up into a fetal position and calmly thought to myself, "I'm going to bleed to death and there is no one who can help. I'd better get ready to die. I'll just curl up right here and die."

As I curled up on the ground, I was struck by an incredible feeling of peace and tranquility. I wasn't in the war zone anymore. I felt as if I'd been totally removed from where my body was lying on the battlefield. The war and my earthly life no longer existed. I was suspended in time and space, between the here-and-now and the here-ever-after.

I still had the sensation of belonging to my body. I was still wounded, but there was no bleeding and no pain. I felt no fear, worry or concern as the darkness enveloped me. I was walking, no, not walking, gliding forward effortlessly at a slight incline, propelled by an unknown force.

I was inside a dark tunnel, a corridor, but I had no sense of anything solid in any direction. It was completely dark all around me, yet I seemed to be aglow with a dim light that emanated from within my heart.

I was bathed in this soft light as I continued to glide forward. As the light washed over me, I felt an incredible sense of calm. I thought for a moment I was dreaming, but there was a far greater sense of being alive than any dream I had ever had. I was completely at ease, even in this highly unusual situation.

Suddenly, I was thrust from the darkness into a bright white light. The White Light surrounded me and at the same time, I was one with the Light. The dim light within me burned brighter and stronger. I no longer possessed my body. I was now a being consisting entirely of Light.

This place of Light was filled with the brightest, purest White Light I had ever seen. It was absolutely pure and clean. It was incredibly warm and friendly. I was in awe. The Light was overwhelming and overshadowed everything else around me. This beautiful Light was filled with goodness and love.

In this incredible bright White Light, everything was beautiful, everything within this Light was totally fulfilling. This place was filled with wonderful love, beautiful, *unconditional* love. It was as though the essence of my being was filled to completion. I had no worry, no fear, no stress, no pressure and no concern about anything. I felt no responsibility for anything. The memory of my entire nineteen-year-old life was slowly fading, diminishing and being replaced by a great sense of universal oneness.

I was a ball of energy...Light energy. I was in a different dimension of existence than I had been on earth. In this dimension, everything was energy based. I'm not sure if the energy came from the Light, or the Light from the energy. This dimension was very unlike the carbon-based dimension I knew on earth.

In this Light-based dimension, I was completely filled with a warm, gentle sense of Spirit. I was awakened to the existence of my soul.

I had only the slightest recollection of what had just happened to me on the battlefield. However, my personality, and the essence of my worldly existence, was still intact. Most of the memories of my life had been muted and my soul and personality were all that was left.

I was full of knowledge of the universe. It wasn't like an academic knowledge. It wasn't like one plus one equals two. It was spiritual knowledge... the meaning of life, where we came from and why we exist. I felt a sense of having great wisdom.

At one point, I was approached by another ball of Light energy which communicated with me. It wasn't a verbal conversation. It was more like a telepathic exchange, an understanding of what was being communicated without using words or voice.

I recognized this Light Being as my grandfather who had died several years before. He told me, "Everything is wonderful here. Allow yourself to be one with the Light."

It was almost as if he put his arm around me, pointed to another part of the Light and continued, saying, "Everything is even more beautiful beyond this point."

We talked for a short time about faith and trusting the Light. He reassured me, saying, "Things are going to be fine, but you must have faith no matter what happens."

I was beginning to see beyond this place of Light. I could see there was a place of great natural beauty beyond us. It was vague, but I sensed there were beautiful, vibrant colors. For a brief moment, I had a picture in my mind of green trees lining a softly flowing, crystal stream. I could almost see a verdant meadow glistening with morning dew. But it was not clear to me exactly where these things were or how I could get to them.

I thought if I kept moving through this bright Light, I would come to an even more beautiful place. After all these years, it is still nearly impossible to find words that adequately describe what I saw in the Light.

A Higher Purpose

While I was conversing with my grandfather and having more heavenly visions, a third ball of energy, like a Spirit Being, came to me. He told me in a stern, but kind voice, "You can't stay here. You must return to your earthly place. When you have fulfilled your higher purpose you will again come to the Light." Like my grandfather, this Spirit Being communicated with me telepathically.

I was hesitant to go back, but He continued to inform me that I must go back to the earthly dimension, fulfill my higher purpose and learn the lessons I would need to successfully journey through the Light. He emphasized that when I had fulfilled my higher purpose and learned my lessons, then, and only then, would I be able to return to this dimension of Light.

I had some concerns about time and space. How was I going to go back where I came from when I no longer existed in that dimension? The Spirit Being assured me in his kind voice, "Time does not exist here and there are no limitations of space."

He told me I would be able to return to this beautiful place and continue this spiritual journey when I had fulfilled my higher purpose. Odd as it sounds, I was told that I would eventually return to this wonderful dimension of Light at precisely the same moment I left it.

I was still a little hesitant, but I heard my grandfather's reassuring voice saying, "It's okay. Have faith in the Spirit." He told me there was no shame in going back. Just because I hadn't achieved what I needed to achieve didn't mean returning to earth was bad or punitive; it was important for me to return to my previous life and do what I was meant to do, to fulfill my higher purpose.

At that moment, for just a moment, it was clear to me what I needed to do. It faded away from me so quickly though, I couldn't fully grasp what it was. However, the knowledge was now part of me. My purpose in life would later be very evident.

Finally, like a good soldier, I obeyed and turned. I was suddenly back in the dark tunnel. I was gliding back in the opposite direction from which I had originally come. My body was full of White Light and glowing brightly. I had a spiritual strength I had never felt before.

Suddenly, I snapped back into my body. The odd thing was, there was no pain. I was still critically injured and bleeding, but I felt no pain.

I had moved through the dark corridor and I was back in Vietnam on the battlefield. I could hear the bombs and the guns and I could hear men screaming, but I felt very calm. I was full of peace and fulfillment, full of this Light and Spirit I had encountered. In fact, I was still glowing with the Light. I was full of Energy, Light Energy. Even though I was back on the battlefield covered in blood and critically injured, I felt incredibly at ease.

I had all of my faculties about me. My senses were heightened and I was acutely aware of everything around me. There was an incredible peace, a spiritual sense of well being I had never experienced before in my life. The Light glowing inside me warmed me with a feeling of peace.

The Fullness of Light

The Spirit was still communicating with me. I knew this combat experience was not over and I would be facing more trauma-filled events. The Spirit assured me I would not die. Regardless of what would happen on this day, I would not die until I had fulfilled my higher purpose in life. I instinctively knew I needed to relax, stay very calm and let the natural flow of life take over. It was as if this Spirit I had experienced in the White Light was within and next to me at the same time. I believed the Light was guiding and directing me. There was also a sense of being protected by the Light.

I started to get up off the ground to go for help when I saw someone come crawling out of the bushes. It was Tommy, the man in my squad I didn't like very well.

He crawled over to me. He'd been shot in the chest and stomach. I took his pack off and saw that his entire back was covered in blood. One of the bullets had gone completely through his body. I knew immediately he was heading for the same place I had just come from.

I took him in my arms, held him tightly and looked into his eyes. I told him everything was going to be all right. I held onto him and we looked each other straight in the eyes. I don't think he saw my wounds. I'm sure all he saw was a caring face. He then gave a short moan and died.

At that moment, all my differences, hostilities and dislike for Tommy dissolved. None of it mattered. I laid him down on the ground and a ball of Energy came up from his body. It appeared as a lightly glowing mist that rose from his head and chest. I spoke telepathically to the ball of energy and said, "You're going to love it there, you're *really* going to love it there. It's a place full of wonder and love and knowledge."

Then, the ball of Energy left him. As I covered Tommy's body with his poncho, I felt a deep bond with him. It was a love and caring that was reserved for special brothers, like John and Hank. To this day, I still feel that love for him and a bond with his soul.

Another Deadly Blow

We were still pinned down by enemy fire. I yelled at my men, "Stay down. I'm going for help."

As I started to get up off the ground, the sniper who had just killed Tommy came out of the tall hedgerow to my left. I watched him step out of the bushes, point his rifle at me and pull the trigger. He opened up on full automatic, his bullets penetrating my upper left arm, chest and neck. I saw the bullets come out of the gun in slow motion and I felt them enter my body, ripping and tearing the flesh. Blood spewed from the wounds. But there was no pain. I felt no fear, worry, panic or concern. I felt only peace and tranquility. The peace from the Light welled up inside me again. Incredibly, I knew there was no need to be alarmed.

I calmly reached over, picked up my rifle, sat up, pointed and fired it in the sniper's direction. I don't think I hit him, but I'm sure I must have scared the living hell out of him. It must have appeared to him that I was the living dead as I lifted myself from a pool of my own blood and aimed my rifle at him.

He had only come out of the bushes to finish me off. He must have been watching as Tommy died in my arms and concluded I was "easy pickin's" since I was seriously wounded.

After he shot me, my left arm was hideously gashed, my chest was ripped open and one of my lungs had collapsed. My throat had gaping holes, my airway was torn and my larynx was severely damaged. What little blood I had left was gushing out all over me again. Still, I had no fear and I felt no pain. I was totally unconcerned because I knew I was *not* going to die!

Guided by the Light

The Spirit of the Light within me became stronger until it was out of my body guiding me. From the Light I heard, "Don't worry about the enemy. The enemy won't bother you anymore." As I stood up, I knew I wouldn't be able to speak because my throat had been badly torn by the sniper's bullets. At this point the Spirit allowed me to see my wounds and guided me in patching them as best I could.

I remembered the words from first-aid training, "To stop the sucking-chest-wound, put your cigarette pack over the hole in your chest." I quickly slapped my cigarette pack over the wound in my chest.

There was nothing to do for my throat, but the Spirit said, "Allow me to help the air go in and keep the blood out."

I could literally see inside of myself and follow the air through my badly torn airway. It went down my throat, into the one lung that was still working and back out. This prevented the blood from filling the good lung.

I knew I had to find help soon because our squad had no medic or radio. I had no idea where the medics were. The Spirit allowed me to envision the entire battlefield so I could see exactly where to go for help. Even though there were tall hedgerows around me, I was able to see in all directions, as if I were standing on my own shoulders.

Suddenly I saw where the medics and radiomen were! The Spirit guided me through the hedges. I remember walking into bushes that were so thick I could barely see light through them.

The Spirit said, "Keep walking. Keep coming forward."

I stepped right *through* the hedgerow—right straight through it! The Spirit guided me through row after row until I came out exactly where the medics, the radiomen and the rest of my company were.

The first guy to approach me was Kurt, a man from one of the other squads. Kurt and I had known each other and had worked together on many occasions. He quickly called the medic when he saw me coming.

When the medic and others from the company came running to help, I heard terrible gasps and groans from the men around me.

"Who is it?" several asked aloud. My face and body were so badly damaged they couldn't even tell who I was until they got closer. Then I heard, "Oh my God, it's Bill!"

When the medic touched me, I felt the Spirit retreat and go back inside of me. I fell to the ground and gave myself over to him. I heard the medic say, "Watch out for that arm! We've got to get an airway started! Give him some morphine!" Everyone was running around in a panic.

Still I remained peaceful and calm. I felt no pain, no fear and no worry because the Spirit had told me that I wasn't going to die. I knew this wasn't the end of my journey. It was just the beginning of a new journey. I knew no matter what happened this day, I would not die.

I had a long way to go, not only to get through whatever physical ordeal was ahead of me, but I also had some higher purpose to fulfill in life. I had to allow the natural path to unfold as I continued with my life. I remember other people talking all around me with so much fear and horror in their voices. I realized my physical appearance incited the horror.

The medic started an IV and had some fluid running into me. He inserted an airway to help keep me breathing. Others packed my wounds with field bandages and strapped my left arm to my chest.

When the medevac helicopter arrived, I was put on a stretcher. Two guys picked me up and while they were loading me on the helicopter, I heard someone say, "There goes one hardcore motherfucker." This was a huge compliment. I was proud I had done my job well and the other men saw me as a strong warrior, a hardcore soldier and a real fighting man.

They finished loading me on the chopper and I was taken away to a field hospital. I was still quite conscious. I breathed a deep sigh of relief that the war was over for me. My only regret was I would never again see my dear friends, John and Hank.

Chapter 8

A Lost Cause

Once on the medevac chopper, I was feeling very thirsty, I motioned to the medic for some water, but he said he couldn't give me anything to drink. Instead, he gave me a wet towel to suck on. This greatly eased my sense of discomfort.

During the transport to the field hospital, I was completely conscious. I remember the flight well. The cool air blowing against my torn and battered body felt very comforting.

Despite my physical condition, I was relaxed and had given myself over to the Spirit. I instinctively knew the Spirit would keep me alive and would not allow any more harm to befall me.

I was quickly flown to the field hospital at LZ Bronco, the closest medical care facility to our position in the field. The casualties were heavy on this particular day and as nurses and doctors passed by me, I heard them remark as they pointed in my direction, "I don't think we can do much with that one."

I was lying naked on a gurney, covered only by a thin white sheet and was being given blood transfusions and whatever else was needed to keep me clinging to life. No one spoke to me. I knew that I was considered a "lost cause" at this point.

The triage team decides who is most salvageable and who is least likely to survive surgery. They determined there were other casualties more likely to make it through surgery than I. They pushed my gurney to a secluded area and I drifted in and out of consciousness. I was very much at peace in this situation. I felt comforted by the Spirit. It was the same sense of comfort I felt as a child when being held in my mother's arms when I was ill or injured.

After what seemed like more than an hour (but was probably more like ten minutes), two men from my company came to where my gurney was parked. I didn't look at them right away, but I could hear them talking to one of the nurses. I heard one of them say, "We're here to identify him."

I turned my head slightly and opened my remaining eye just enough to see them. My face was swollen and I was so doped-up I could barely move. I recognized the faces of a lieutenant from the company and our company clerk; both of them knew me quite well. I looked at them, but I couldn't respond.

They were hesitant to get close, but I heard the lieutenant say, "Yeah, that's him," and they hastily left.

I thought, "They don't understand. They think I am dying or already dead!" In my mind I screamed, "*I'm not dead, I'm alive!*" I tried to speak but nothing came out.

I don't know how long I was left on the gurney, but it seemed like a very long time. Finally, a medic came out and said, "He's still alive!"

I was taken inside where some minor procedures were performed. I heard the doctor say, "Well, there's not much more we can do for him here. Let's stabilize him and send him up to Chu Lai."

Chu Lai was about 60 miles North from Duc Pho and LZ Bronco. It was a much larger base with a well-equipped hospital.

When I arrived in Chu Lai, the doctor said, "There's not much we can do here. Keep him stable and we'll send him to

Da Nang." Da Nang was about 60 or 70 miles North of Chu Lai and had an even better hospital.

Once in Da Nang, I was told I would be sent to a hospital ship in Da Nang Harbor. They helicoptered me to the deck of the U.S.S. Repose. The medical people were now keeping me informed of where I was going and what would be happening next. I was still very calm and relaxed.

It was starting to get dark outside as they carried me from the helicopter to the emergency room on the ship. Nighttime in the war zone was always a frightening time but I felt safe on the ship. Once in the emergency room, they carefully lifted me onto an examination table.

After half a day's worth of helicopter travel, I was a bit uncomfortable and so I motioned to the medic that I wanted to sit up. It was hard to breathe when I was lying down. I thought I would feel much more comfortable sitting up. My body was starting to feel the stress of the traumatic events of the day. The tracheotomy tube that was installed in my neck back at LZ Bronco was uncomfortable and I wasn't used to breathing through it yet. I had been lying down all day and I wanted to sit up so I could breath easier. I was never very good at charades, but the medic got the message.

Dead Man Sitting

As the doctor walked into the room, the medic was telling me he wasn't sure I should be sitting up, but said he would ask the doctor. The doctor looked at me in astonishment, shook his head and motioned to the medic to help me sit up. As I sat on the edge of his exam table, the doctor paced back and forth in front of me shaking his head.

Finally, he looked at me and said, "I don't believe this. You *should* be dead. What are you doing *sitting* on my table?" He shook his head, threw up his hands and said, "I don't even know where to start."

The doctor discussed the need for x-rays with the other medical staff, suggesting there were probably bullets still lodged in my brain. I overheard him talking about bullets in the brain. Since I was unable to speak, I quickly motioned for a pen and paper so I could write a note letting him know what had happened to me. I simply wrote, "No bullets in brain."

I had to convince him my head wounds were from a bomb blast, not bullets. After writing several notes, he was finally convinced the head injuries were from a bomb blast and the arm, chest and neck injuries were gunshot wounds.

I was getting a little excited so the doctor said, "It's okay. We understand now. Just lie back down and we'll take care of you." I lay back down and let them do what they needed to do.

The medics prepped me for surgery by shaving me from the top of my head all the way to my waist. I'm a pretty hairy guy so this was a big job. The last thing I remember before being wheeled to the operating room was the anesthesiologist giving me a shot. As he administered the injection he said, "You're a very lucky young man."

I smiled and thought, "Luck had nothing to do with it. The Spirit saved me."

The Light That Shined

I don't know how long I was unconscious after surgery, maybe a day or two. When I regained consciousness, I was in the ship's intensive care ward. When I opened my eyes, the light was so bright I thought I was back in the Spirit World.

One of the nurses noticed I was conscious and came over to comfort me. She said she would tell the doctor I was awake so he could come see me.

When the doctor arrived, the first thing he did was check my vision. He took his penlight, unwrapped some of the bandages on my head, shined the light in one eye and said, "Can you see that?"

I responded, "Yes" by nodding my head.

He shined the light in the other eye and said, "Can you see that?"

Again, I nodded, "Yes."

I knew I had only one good eye, but I imagined I saw the light in both eyes. I wanted to say something to the doctor, but I couldn't speak because of the injuries to my neck. It was a strange feeling not being able to speak.

Although I was not able to verbalize my thoughts, I never stopped speaking in my head. I never thought that I couldn't speak, only that I couldn't make the words come out of my mouth. The doctor finished his exam and went off to consult with some of the other physicians.

A short time later, several doctors came by and I made a writing motion with my hand indicating I wanted a pen and pad to write notes. My first note to them said, "I want to stand up and go to the bathroom."

The doctor in charge took the note and quickly read it. He said, "No, no, no, you can't go to the bathroom!"

I nodded my head yes and wrote him a note saying, "Yes, yes, I want to go to the bathroom. I want to take a pee."

He said, "No, no. You're catheterized. It will just happen."

I wrote back, "No catheter! I want to pee!" I insisted that they remove the catheter and threatened to remove it myself if they didn't take it out immediately. They finally gave in and the nurse took the catheter out.

I had IV tubes in my one good arm and was bandaged from the waist up like a mummy. While the doctors watched, two nurses stood me up next to the bed and another held a bedpan in front of me while I tried to urinate. It took a while and it was hard to get a stream started with so many people watching me, but I finally peed.

When I finished, the nurses helped me back to bed and brought me a can of Coca-Cola, which I thought was rather odd. The doctor said the Coke would help to keep me from being nauseated.

As I slowly sipped on the Coke, the doctors came back to my bedside. They unwrapped the bandages on my head and one of the doctors said, "Bill, we have some really bad news for you. We weren't able to save your right eye."

I thought, "Well, I already knew that." I had watched most of my right eye drop out into my helmet on the battlefield so I wasn't surprised or shocked. I just shrugged, no big deal.

The doctor continued, "Well, we thought maybe you didn't know. When Dr. Smith shined the flashlight in your eyes, you said you saw light in both eyes."

I *had* seen light in both eyes. But the light I saw was the light in my mind, not from the flashlight. I wrote the doctor a note telling him I *had* seen light in both eyes, but I knew they didn't understand what I was trying to tell them. I wasn't even sure I understood.

The doctor went on with his bad news, telling me I would never speak again and there was still a good chance I might lose my left arm. He said I would not be able to breathe without a tracheotomy tube in my neck. He went on to tell me they would do everything possible to help, but because of the severity of my injuries, I would most likely be disabled for the rest of my life.

The doctor painted a very pessimistic picture of my ability to recover, but in my heart, I knew he was wrong. The doctor said it was a miracle I was still alive. He was astounded that I had wanted to get out of bed and pee.

I wanted to tell someone about my incredible experience in the Light and about the Spirit that continued to fill me so completely, but I couldn't speak. The experience seemed so far removed from this dimension and it was so indescribable. The doctors and nurses tended to me without an inkling of the Great Spirit within me. Concerned only with healing my broken body, they remained oblivious to the spiritual energy healing me. They were blinded by their own reality, unable to comprehend the full power of the Spirit that was operating within me.

Now that I was awake, I wanted to be able to get up and walk around. The doctors kept saying, "No, no, no, you're going to be here for a long time and you just need to stay in bed."

I kept telling them, "No, I can't. I need to be up. I wanna be up." My Spirit was restless and I knew that getting up and moving around would be a healthy thing for me. I persisted in my requests to sit up and get out of bed.

The doctors finally conceded and said, "Well, if he wants to get up, get him up and put him on a ward." So I was taken out of intensive care long before the doctors wanted me to leave. I was put on a regular ward with soldiers, sailors and marines whose injuries were minor compared to mine.

From A Spirit Perspective

The hospital ward on the ship was a bit different from a regular hospital ward. The beds were actually bunks stacked three high, with safety rails on the sides. The bunks were suspended by vertical rails that ran floor to ceiling at each corner of the bunk. Of course, due to my condition, I was on a bottom bunk. My bunk was at the opposite end of the ward from the head (the Navy word for bathroom).

Instinctively, I knew I had to get up and move around a little. It was really, really hard to stand up by myself and walk, but I knew, no matter how difficult, I had to get up. It was like the Spirit kept a steady flow of thoughts going through my mind. Not audible words, but more like an intuition that constantly motivated me. The Spirit kept prodding me to get up, move around and go to the head.

The doctors and nurses kept telling me, "No, no, no. You're not supposed to get up and move around. If you have to go to the toilet you can use a bedpan. Please rest for a few more days."

I could understand their concern. From a purely physical standpoint, my wounds were so extensive, so serious and so deep they weren't even able to stitch them up yet. In fact, it would be almost a month before they would even attempt to stitch my wounds closed. But I was operating from a different perspective - a spiritual perspective - one that defied the physical. Therefore, I kept getting out of bed and moving around near my bunk. I would hold on to the side of the bunk to steady myself, all to the consternation of the doctors and medical staff. My goal was to be able to get up and walk to the head without assistance.

With A Little Help From The Spirit

I continued to work on my goal of getting to the head unassisted. The nurse on the ward was a helpful fellow, but I didn't want his help. I wanted to make my first journey to the head all on my own.

Besides the most obvious obstacles, the hospital ship constantly swayed. It moved gently back and forth, all day long. To say I had a difficult time gaining my equilibrium was an understatement, but I was determined to get out of bed and pee in a toilet like a normal person.

After two days of practice and reluctantly using a bedpan, I decided to go for it. My left arm was strapped to my chest with bandages so I only had one arm to steady myself. I wobbled down the pathway to the head, clinging to bunks and walls along the way.

On the ship, some of the doorways were like hatches that did not open from floor to ceiling. When I got to the entrance of the head there was a six-inch lip I had to step over. This was an additional hurdle to overcome. With much effort, I managed to get into the head and up to the urinal. I stood there holding the rail next to the urinal with my right hand, wondering how I was going to steady myself and pee without dribbling all over.

Leaning on the rail, I struggled to hold myself up and pee at the same time. It was quite a balancing act, but I did it, all by myself - with a little help from the Spirit. The nurse on duty commented, "Watching you walk to the head is the most amazing thing I've ever seen." I had told him not to try to help me unless I fell down and couldn't get back up.

I had been making this trip to the head a couple of times a day when the nurse said, "You know, by all that I know medically, you should not even be out of bed. In fact, you should probably still be in intensive care." He continued, "But you're up and you're walking. Some of these other guys are hardly wounded at all and they won't get up and go to the head. They use the bedpan."

I couldn't respond verbally, so I just shrugged. I thought to myself, "The Spirit continues to tell me this is what I have to do. I have to normalize myself. I have to get up and go to the bathroom everyday. I can't be concerned about how others might deal with such injuries." Getting up and going to the head every day, no matter how difficult, was the most normal thing I could think of to do.

One night a new night-duty nurse came to change the bandages on my left arm. I had seen her on the ward before in the day, but this was the first time she changed my bandages.

She shuttered when she looked at my wounds. She tried not to let me see the look on her face, but I noticed her grimace.

The skin on my upper left arm and chest was split about four to five inches wide and open all the way down to the bone. The flesh and muscle were gone and the wounds were wide open. The nurse took the packing out, cleaned the wounds, applied medication and packed the whole thing back together.

She looked at me and shook her head. She said, "I know this wound is terrible, but what really amazes me is the first time I walked into this ward, you reached out with THAT arm (pointing to my damaged arm), grabbed the bars and pulled yourself up out of bed. When I took the bandages off and looked at your wounds, I was astounded. I couldn't believe you did that with the damage to your arm."

A large part of me was still functioning in the spiritual dimension so physical limitations did not seem relevant to accomplishing my goals. The driving force was my Spirit, not my body or my mind. If left to the devices of logic and clinical proof, I would have thought myself completely helpless, dependent on doctors and nurses to heal me and make me normal again. There seemed to be no preoccupation with pain or physical inability. I was directed by the Spirit, and the thoughts of being helpless or disabled were pretty much non-existent.

I was still spending most of my time in bed, but I tried to get out of bed and sit in a wheelchair for an hour or so each day. I was also making my shaky walk to the head once or twice a day. The medical staff was very attentive and saw that I was well cared for. I was bathed and had my bandages changed twice a day.

Humor That Heals

I don't remember how long I had been on the ward when this next incident happened. It still makes me laugh. I was wrapped with gauze from above my waist all the way up to the top of my head, with just my mouth, nose, and one eye showing. I was one big bandage with my left arm strapped to my chest. I was sitting against a wall in a wheelchair looking pretty pathetic. I looked like a very battle-worn soldier. The next thing I knew, a Marine Corps General strutted onto the ward.

He walked around, with his chest puffed out, passing out medals to all the marines. He bellowed out, "I'm so proud of you boys." Some of these guys had little tiny nicks, nothing really – just flesh wounds. But it was show time for the general and he walked around telling them how proud he was of his marines. He carried on as if he were addressing a roomful of Medal of Honor winners.

I sat there taking it all in as the general passed out medals, shook hands and made his rounds. He hadn't spotted me yet. I was in the corner away from the marines. He went up and down the row of bunks with his entourage.

When he saw me sitting in the corner, his eyes lit up and his expression said, "Oh boy, I got a real hero here!" He strode over and said, "I'm gonna give you a medal, boy." He then asked, in his most pompous manner, "What unit are you with, son?"

I motioned him down so I could whisper in his ear. With a look of great expectation on his face, the general moved closer.

When he got his ear near my mouth, I mustered all the energy I could and gently whispered in his ear, "Army!"

Realizing I wasn't a marine, he took a step back and looked at me incredulously. The general stood there for a moment with his mouth open and didn't say another word. Then he quickly turned on his heel and left.

I had a huge grin on my face and chuckled to myself for twenty minutes afterward. He never did give me a medal.

Feed the Spirit

The entire time I was on the hospital ship, I wasn't allowed to have any solid food. After I was moved to the ward from the ICU, they removed the IV tubes that were supplying me with nutrition. They told me I could now take nutrition by mouth. I was looking forward to some real good food!

At first, I was only allowed broth. They gave me broth for breakfast, broth for lunch and more broth for dinner. I was getting good at writing notes so I asked, "Can't I get something better?"

They replied, "Well, we could give you some Jell-O."

Then I got red Jell-O for breakfast, red Jell-O for lunch and red Jell-O for dinner.

I was getting fed-up with this single-mindedness about food. Again, I wrote a note and asked, "Can't I have something else? Can't I have some *real* food?"

So they gave me chicken noodle soup. It was a little thicker, with a little more substance to it. However, three meals a day of chicken noodle soup was not what I had in mind either.

They were getting closer to something resembling solid food, so I suffered along with it. Then I was upgraded to soup *and* Jell-O, but I was ravenously hungry for something more substantial. The Spirit inside continued to tell me I could eat whatever I was hungry for, but the doctors weren't listening to my Spirit. I had long, detailed dreams about food, especially breakfast! My dreams were so vivid I could almost taste the bacon and eggs.

I told them I wanted to get up and go to the mess hall with the rest of the guys. Some of the guys on the ward had told me how good the food was in the mess hall. The Spirit constantly prodded me to get up and move around. I thought eating at the mess hall would be great. But the staff refused my request. They said, "There's no way you can eat anything more solid."

I said, in writing, "Yeah? I can eat whatever I want. No problem. Take me to the mess hall and I'll show you." I never won that battle. I never got to eat in the mess hall or have "real" food while on the hospital ship.

After several weeks I was ready to leave the ship and go to Japan for additional treatment and stabilization before embarking on the long journey home. The first stop was a holding area at the hospital in Da Nang. The holding area was nothing more than a series of Quonset huts with hospital beds lined up against the walls.

As they wheeled me in, I waited for them to make up a bed for me. This holding area was where all the wounded in this sector were held between transfers to other medical facilities for additional treatment or sent back to the States. Consequently, there were a lot of wounded men coming and going.

It was just before lunchtime when they put me in a bed. Then a lunch tray arrived. In fact, it was a *very* nice lunch. When

I opened the tray, I saw real food: meat, baked potato and all the trimmings.

I thought, "Somehow I will manage to get this meal down." I knew it wasn't *my* lunch. It had been intended for the previous patient. Too bad! I quickly ate the whole thing. I certainly wasn't going to tell them to send it back!

I chewed and chewed and chewed on the meat until I was able to swallow it. The potatoes and veggies went down a little easier. Best of all was the desert, a small square of chocolate cake with a little powdered sugar sprinkled on top. I ate the entire meal in less than ten minutes.

When the nurse came back, she looked at the tray, then looked at me and said, "That wasn't your tray, was it?"

As I shook my head "No," I had a huge grin on my face.

She smiled, shook her head and said, "You're a bad boy."

I nodded my head in agreement.

She said, "You were supposed to eat soup."

I wrote a quick note, "I'm sick of soup."

The nurse replied, "I think we need to tell the doctor you're ready for some solid food."

In the end, all I got was vegetable soup and mashed potatoes. Still not what I was looking for.

Chapter 9

The Second Battle for Food

After a day and a half in Da Nang, I was finally deemed stable enough to be sent to Japan. They said I would be sent to an Army base there called Camp Drake. I was told it had a very good hospital. Before they put me on the plane to Japan, they once again put me on intravenous feeding.

On arrival in Japan I was back to square one, still on the IV receiving only liquid foods until a doctor would give the order to change my diet. I was placed on a large open ward with thirty beds. The ward was an oblong room with double doors at one end and a glassed-in nurses station at the other end. My bed was against an outside wall with windows at my head that looked out over a small, grassy yard and a paved street. Across the street was a long eggshell-colored building, but it didn't appear to be a hospital building. It may have been a warehouse or office building.

The latrine was through a door about thirty feet directly across the ward from my bed. I had my sights set on getting up and going to the latrine as soon as possible. But if I wanted to get out of bed, I had to drag the IV pole wherever I went.

Shortly after I was settled, I got out of bed to go to the bathroom. I was pushing my IV pole toward the latrine when I heard a nurse bellow, "What the hell are you doing?"

I got out my little note pad and wrote him a note, "I'm going to the bathroom."

He said loudly, as if giving an order, "You're NOT supposed to be out of bed."

I argued with him and wrote, "But I'm going to the bathroom!" I stuck out the note and just moved on. I went ahead and took care of my business.

On my way back to bed, he said, "We're going to give you a bath. I don't think you've had a bath in a while."

I penned another note. "I'm going to shower later."

He scowled, "I don't think so."

I wrote, "Yes, I'm going to shower later!" I had not yet taken a shower on my own, but this guy was pissing me off so I decided I would do it just to spite him.

Eventually the nurse gave up and said he would tell the doctor about my difficult behavior.

Later I went to the latrine and I stood in the shower without getting myself too wet in the wrong places, but I showered. I was very careful because my arm and chest wounds were still completely open. The nurses had a fit because I wouldn't behave like a totally disabled person, but I think they also admired my Spirit, as they didn't try very hard to stop me from moving about.

The Hamburger Spirit

The next day the doctor ordered the IV removed and put me on a soft, bland diet. I went through the same arguments about the meals as I did on the ship, but I was able to convince them to give me a little bit more solid food. They gave me mashed potatoes and gravy, steamed vegetables and other soft foods, but I craved meals that are more substantial. I wanted meat. As odd as it sounds, I instinctively knew I could eat the same food the other patients were eating. Again, I was operating from a Spirit perspective in the midst of, and in defiance of, medical assumptions and limitations.

After several days in the hospital at Camp Drake, I was getting up and moving around a little better. It was still a struggle to go the bathroom though. I could only stay out of bed for ten or fifteen minutes at a time before tiring.

One particularly lovely day, the nurse suggested I get in a wheelchair and have someone push me outside to get some fresh air. She knew I couldn't go far on my own because I only had the use of one arm. It was wonderful to be outside in the bright sunshine, especially since I was no longer in the war zone.

While I was sitting outside enjoying the sweet smell of fresh air, another aroma peaked my interest. One of the patients, still dressed in his pajamas and hospital robe, came walking up the sidewalk holding a small cardboard box filled with hamburgers and French fries. The smell of the freshly cooked burgers and greasy fries made my mouth water. I got his attention and wrote a quick note, asking him where he got the burgers.

He told me there was a little hamburger joint on base, just up the road from the hospital. "Hmmm," I thought, "If I could get someone to push me up the road, I could get to the hamburger stand."

Later that evening, in the presence of the nurses, I ate my soup and mashed potatoes. Then, I got someone to push me up the road to the hamburger stand where I got a burger, fries and a chocolate shake. This was heaven! This was the first hamburger I had enjoyed since leaving home more than ten months earlier.

As long as I chewed well, eating the burger was no trouble. I no longer needed to do battle with the doctors to get solid food from the hospital. I knew I would be visiting this little piece of nirvana again soon.

From The Medical Perspective

From the doctor's perspective, I was not expected to live. I was continually warned I was very fragile and could take a turn for the worse at any time.

I remember thinking, "These people are awfully negative! Don't they know I'm going to be okay?" I knew I would not die, I was confident in the guidance the Spirit was giving me.

There was one doctor, Captain Miller, who was a little more optimistic. He took the time to have some long talks with me. I briefly told him of my out of body experience and let him know the Spirit was still with me. He seemed to understand. He wanted to do some surgery on my neck and informed me they would be closing the wounds on my chest and arm at the same time.

The next morning I was prepped to go to surgery. The nurse gave me a quick sponge bath and dressed me in an open-backed hospital gown. She gave me a shot of Demerol that made me feel like I was floating on a cloud.

When the two men dressed in surgical scrubs brought the gurney to take me to the operating room, the nurse asked me where my personal belongings were so she could lock them in the safe. I told her they were in my nightstand. I was then whisked off to the operating room.

When I got to the operating room, Dr. Miller was there and explained he was going to take some skin grafts from my legs. He said he would use the grafts to patch some of the damaged areas inside my throat. I was pretty high on the Demerol and agreed to everything he said.

The surgery went well and I spent a few hours in recovery before being moved back to my bed on the ward. Dr. Miller came to my bedside when I was coherent again and discussed what had been done. He informed me that huge, thick, steel sutures had been used to pull my chest and arm wounds together. He said it had been quite an ordeal to pull the wounds together, but he believed they would heal well with the proper attention. Dr. Miller also warned there was still a slight chance I might lose my left arm. He said the likelihood it would be a fully functional limb was slim.

Dr. Miller saved the bad news for last. He informed me the damage to my larynx was worse than anticipated. Although he had used the skin grafts to reconstruct my airway, he said my vocal cords were damaged beyond repair. That meant I would never be able to speak again. He said even though they were able to patch my airway, it was still only about half the size of normal. He told me that meant I would not be able to breathe normally without the tracheotomy tube.

I already knew I was severely injured and that these injuries would affect me for a lifetime so the doctor's statements did not particularly alarm me. I was still in denial about the severity of my injuries. Although the Spirit was guiding me during these difficult times, I was not yet fully aware that I would always have to cope with the human frailties of life, just like any other human being. The Spirit could give me the will to live, but it couldn't take away the fact that my body was irreparably broken.

Complications

After the surgery, I didn't sleep well and was in some pain from the procedures. I was having night sweats and bad dreams. Within a couple days, the sutures in my left arm got infected and started tearing the skin, leaving large gashes perpendicular to the wound. Then the wound began pulling apart.

The doctor came to me and said, "We may have to amputate your left arm." Because of the infection, they wanted to cut off my left arm. I couldn't believe what I was hearing. He said because of the severe damage to the muscles, in all likelihood, I would not be able to use it again anyway. He told me my arm would, most likely, just hang lifeless at my side.

I kept writing notes and shaking my head saying, "No. You're wrong." I just knew it would be all right. The doctor had doubts about my ability to heal, but I had no such doubts at this time. As long as there was even the slightest chance of recovery, I wanted to take the chance. The Spirit continually affirmed my destiny to live and to fulfill my higher purpose in life. I refused to allow the amputation of my arm, or my Spirit.

At this time, I wasn't exactly sure what my higher purpose was, but I knew I had one. I knew at some point I would more clearly recognize it. My main concern was just to get healthy enough to do whatever would come next.

In terms of language and clear thoughts, these spiritual messages were somewhat vague because they were not readily translated into human terms. The Spirit doesn't necessarily speak English and the messages were not always as clear as I would have liked them to be.

Looking back, I realize the higher purpose at that moment was to heal my body as much as possible so I would be able to carry out the greater mission of my higher purpose.

There continued to be complications to my recovery and additional physical challenges to overcome. Besides the infection in my arm, my chest and neck were now infected. The doctors worked hard to combat the infections, but my body seemed to be losing strength. I was feeling physically weakened. It was very different from how I'd been feeling up to this point.

I thought, "Things are going downhill quickly and I'm not doing very well."

They put me back on the intravenous feeding and the doctors and nurses began to monitor me more carefully.

A Drastic Measure

I kept getting worse. The Spirit within was strong, but my body was weak. I knew there was something more than the infection making me ill. I told the nurse, "Something's terribly wrong. I'm not doing well."

She took my temperature and it was up to 103 degrees! She said, "Well, maybe it's just the infection."

They started to work harder on getting the infection under control by increasing the dosages of antibiotics and other medications. However, the fever refused to relent.

Soon, I became delirious. The doctors determined that, on top of everything else, I had contracted malaria. Malaria is a very painful and discomforting disease, not to mention that it is also life threatening. My body ached all the way to my bones. My skin was so sensitive it was painful just to feel my hair lying against it. I can remember lying in bed, completely soaked from head to toe in my own perspiration. The sheets had to be changed every hour.

The nurse came in and said, "If your fever doesn't go down soon we're going to have to take drastic measures to get it down. Your fever is getting dangerously high."

I had no idea what she meant by "drastic measures." At this point, my temperature was 105 degrees and it continued to stay at 105 degrees.

The nurse left my bed and was back in a few minutes with an entourage. They lifted me out of bed and sat me in a wheel chair. I was only semi-conscious as they lifted me from the bed. Although they were gentle, the pain of being touched was almost unbearable.

I was taken to the tub room located next to the nurses station. The nurses stripped me naked and lowered me into a bathtub partially filled ice cubes. If I could have screamed, I would have.

Then they rubbed me down with alcohol and put more ice on top of me. I was in agony. I was sure I was going back to the White Light and it would have been extremely welcome at that moment. I passed out before they could remove me from the tub. The next morning I awoke in my hospital bed.

Of all the injuries, pain and procedures I had experienced, the ice bath was the most excruciating. I can't remember anything as painful since, but the bath of alcohol and ice cubes worked. My fever broke. I continued to battle the severe symptoms of the malaria for nearly a week. My already battered and beaten body worked overtime to fight the disease.

During the battle with malaria, the infection in my wounds worsened. There were long tears around the wounds where the metal wires had pulled through my rotting flesh and the doctors had to remove the wire sutures from my wounds until the infection healed.

When I had healed from both the infection and the malaria, the doctors were absolutely stunned. They said, "Most men would have died from such an ordeal, especially on top of your existing injuries. You have an amazing constitution. I wish we knew where that kind of strength comes from."

I knew. There was always the Spirit sustaining me. I wanted to try explaining it to them but it was impossible. How could I explain to these medical professionals that regardless of what was happening to my physical body, my Spiritual body was strong. The Spirit gave me the will and the energy to continue against worldly odds.

Destined to Live

I was still weak from my battle with malaria and a bit overconfident about my ability to survive whatever ailment befell me. It was early evening. I was sitting up in bed just after my soft food dinner. I saw two men in surgical scrubs pushing a gurney in my direction.

They were bringing a new patient on the ward. He looked awful. They put him in the bed right across from mine.

A few minutes later, one of the nurses came over to me and asked, "In the morning, would you go and talk to that guy across from you? He's in about the same condition as you were when you first arrived and his wounds are very similar to yours. I think if he could see how you deal with this, it might help him to heal."

I told her I would go and see him in the morning.

The next morning when I awoke, I looked over and his bed was empty. A nurse came by and I jotted a quick note, "Where's the guy who came in last night?"

She said, "He didn't make it. He passed during the night."

It suddenly struck me how serious my injuries were and reminded me how fragile life can be. This guy didn't even make it through the night. He could have made it through the night, but he didn't, and I did. The only difference was I had the confidence that I would not die. It was my destiny to live, no matter how disabled I might be.

Another Loss

I was gaining strength after the great ordeal with malaria and infection and I pleaded with Dr. Miller to put me on a regular diet. After telling him about the Hamburger Spirit, he agreed to change my diet to solid foods.

I was ecstatic. Finally, I was going to get some real food on a regular basis. This also meant when I was able, I could walk to the hamburger stand and get a burger and fries without hiding it from the nurses.

I was actually getting around on foot fairly well now and the medical staff had stopped complaining about my frequent trips to the latrine. As I was walking past the nurses station on my way to take a shower one night, I saw a scale and decided to weigh myself.

I was astonished. I weighed 128 pounds. I was 180 pounds of muscle and blood when I left for Vietnam. I hadn't realized how emaciated I had become from all the illness and injury. I had always been a big strong kid, a little overweight, but muscular. I decided I had better start eating more and exercising.

The next morning was warm and sunny and I knew I needed to go for a walk outside. This seemed like a great day to try walking to the hamburger stand. I decided to skip lunch on the ward and make the trek. This would be the longest walk I would make since my injuries.

When I went to get my money from the bag in my nightstand so I could buy a burger, I remembered the nurse had locked it up in the safe when I went to surgery. They couldn't find my bag at the nurses station and said it must have gotten sent to the post security office.

The security office was near the hamburger stand. I thought I would walk there and get my lunch on the way back. The MP at the security office could find no record of my bag being checked with them.

I went back to the nurses station and asked them to double check. No luck. My bag, with what few personal things I had left, was missing.

I was devastated. There wasn't much in the bag—my military ID, Geneva Convention Card, $30-$40 in cash and a letter from home, but it was all I had. Now I had nothing.

There was some buzz around the ward that the nurse who took my bag for safekeeping had stolen the money and dumped the bag. She was scheduled to go home the day following my surgery and someone said she had money problems. From what I understood, other patients had reported personal items missing around the time she left. I trusted my life to the doctors and nurses and didn't want to believe a nurse would do such a thing.

I never found out what happened to my personal possessions, but it was another in a long series of emotional loses I had to absorb.

I began to understand that just because an angel had touched me, it didn't mean I wouldn't have to dance with the devil from time to time. The Spirit could only go so far to protect me in this dimension. After all, I was, and still am, fully human and subject to the same human experience as any other human being.

Word from the Field

The Army was kind enough to give me an advance on my pay when the head nurse informed the paymaster of my financial loss.

I once again set out to get a hamburger. I was still bandaged from the waist up. My chest and arm wounds were still open and healing from the infection. I had to be careful when I went outside and make sure I was properly bandaged and dressed in pajamas and a robe. The nurses had learned not to challenge me when I decided to do something they thought might not be medically prudent.

I made it to the hamburger stand and back without incident. As I sat on my bed finishing the last of my chocolate shake, I looked up to see a wheelchair being pushed onto the ward. The soldier in the chair had a familiar face–it was Danny!

Danny was a guy from my platoon, a man I trusted and had fought side by side with on many occasions. It was odd to see him here. I had almost forgotten about Vietnam and my friends back in the war. Danny had a gauze patch over his left eye, but other than that he looked to be in good shape. I got out of my bed and walked over to his bedside.

As soon as he saw me, he sat up and grabbed my good arm. He recognized me immediately and said, "My God, I thought you were dead. They told us that they didn't expect you to live."

I couldn't speak, but I squeezed his hand and grinned. I got out my notepad and quickly scribbled a note, "What are you doing here?"

He told me he had a grenade fragment in his eye and would only be here for a day or two. He said they had sent him here because the surgery to remove the fragment was a delicate job and they didn't have the facilities available in Vietnam.

Danny told me the guys in my company missed me. He said John and Hank were extremely upset when they heard I had been killed while they were on R&R.

I thought about how I might feel if one of them had been killed while I was away. I couldn't imagine what they were going through, the guilt they must have felt when they found out I was killed while they were having a good time. I told Danny to be sure and tell them I was all right, and I would be going home soon.

Danny could plainly see I was not all right, but he knew what I meant. I didn't want John and Hank to be concerned about me. They had enough to think about to keep themselves alive long enough to go home.

I spent the rest of the day sitting next to Danny's bed talking and playing cards. It was great to finally have someone to talk to who had been in combat with me. That night I was tired and slept well for the first time since I had been hospitalized.

The next day Danny walked to the hamburger stand with me at lunchtime. When we returned the nurse approached us and let us know Danny would be going back to Vietnam the next morning.

I was sad he would be leaving but even sadder he would be going back to a place where he might be killed or more severely wounded. I was worried about John and Hank. I wanted to be there for them, or at least send my Spirit to watch over them.

I started feeling guilty I was in a nice warm bed every night while my friends faced the perils of combat everyday and slept in the dirt. I was eating hamburgers and fries while they were eating C-rations.

Part of me wanted to heal quickly and return to the war. I realized that I missed the adrenaline rush of a hard-fought firefight. Yet, I didn't want to go back to the fear and danger or suffer being wounded again. In my heart, I knew my military career was over, but in my head, I was still a warrior.

Writing Home to Mom

Dr. Miller took me to surgery one more time to close my wounds. This time there was no infection and the wounds began to heal. He instructed the nurses to change the dressings twice a day and scrub the wounds with peroxide.

While recovering at Camp Drake, I thought a lot about going home. I remember being frightened to send a letter to my mother because I didn't want her to know how badly I had been wounded. I believed I had let her down and felt ashamed to tell her that I was not going to come home healthy.

Before I left for Vietnam I told her, "I'm coming back, Mom, and I'm coming back in one piece." I promised her I wouldn't get hurt. "I'll be careful, Mom."

But when you go off to war and tell your mom you're not going to get hurt, it's a little different than telling her that you'll be careful and look both ways when crossing the street. War is simply not like that. There are certain promises that are impossible to keep. I was a good soldier. I went to Vietnam with every intention of coming home unscathed. I wanted to survive–and I still got wounded.

I was slowly becoming aware that my wounds were part of my destiny and part of my higher purpose in life, but that would not ease my mother's pain. I knew the Army had notified my family by now that I had been injured and my mom would be grievously worried about me.

I wanted to write home, but I didn't have the energy. Writing letters was never my strong point. In Vietnam, I would use carbon paper to make copies of my generic letters and send them to everyone on my mailing list.

One day while Dr. Miller was checking my wounds, he asked if I had written home yet. I told him no. He said the Red Cross had notified him that my parents had contacted the Department of the Army and wanted some direct contact with me. He informed me that a Red Cross volunteer would come by in the afternoon and help me write a letter home. I was relieved I would finally make contact with my family, but felt extremely guilty I had gotten wounded.

As I thought about what to say in my letter, the guilt and shame overwhelmed me. I felt like a failure. I wasn't sure I could face my family and friends. It wasn't just being wounded I was worried about. I was a completely different person than I had been when I last saw them. The carnage I had experienced in war was permanently life changing.

In the last year, I had grown from being a boy to being a man, in a very ugly way. The wounds from this war were not all visible. The worst of them were those held in my mind. Many thoughts of bloody battles came flooding back, and I wept.

Later that afternoon the Red Cross worker showed up at my bedside. She was a very plain looking, middle-aged woman with mousy brown hair and a thin smile. She seemed somewhat detached, like she wanted to help me but didn't want to know me. It was as if the only personality she possessed was that of being a Red Cross volunteer.

She pulled up a chair and got right to business. In a clinical tone she asked, "What would you like to say to your family?"

I jotted a quick note on my notepad saying, "Just tell them I'm okay and I'll be home soon."

She started writing on her Red Cross stationary. She wrote a very nice letter explaining I had been wounded in combat and was now at Camp Drake Army Hospital. She noted my spirits were high as I was recovering from my injuries and I would be returning home soon.

It was a short letter, but covered all the bases. When she finished, she handed me the letter to read and asked me to sign the bottom. As soon as I handed it back to her with my shaky signature on the bottom, she stood up and said she would mail the letter immediately.

Dr. Miller had taught me I could speak in a whisper if I put my finger over the hole in my tracheotomy tube. He had instructed me to do it only when I really needed to speak. As she stood there, I put my finger over the hole and whispered, "Thank you." She gave a glimpse of a sweet personality as she smiled down on me, then she turned and walked away.

I was relieved the letter was done and some of the guilt and shame washed away. But I couldn't help feeling like I had failed my family and friends by not being the same person I was when I had last seen them. Life was perfect when I was completely engulfed by the Spirit, but after coming back to the material world I had strong emotions to deal with. I wanted to let go and be in the Spirit world, but the human world kept tugging at me.

Going Home

I had been in Japan for nearly two months. Finally, the day was coming when I would be going back to the States. Dr. Miller came to me on the ward and said, "Bill, I think we have done all we can to help you. I believe you are strong enough to make the trip home now."

I couldn't believe I was actually going home. I was frightened. I knew I had a long road to recovery ahead of me and I didn't know what to expect when I got home. I still had nearly two years left on my enlistment contract. I was wondering how the Army would deal with my physical disability.

The doctors made it clear they didn't think I would be able to function as a normal person and expected me to be hospitalized for a very long time. I still had a tracheotomy tube in my throat and my face was still crushed. They had put a plastic retainer in my empty eye socket and there were hundreds of stitches holding the right side of my face together. Although they saved my left arm it was not very functional and I still tired very easily when up and about.

That night I made one last trip to the hamburger stand and had my usual burger, fries and chocolate shake. I didn't sleep well. I was worried about the trip home and what I would say to my family when I saw them. As morning broke I couldn't sleep, so I got up and showered, shaved and put on clean pajamas and a robe for the trip home.

I sat up in bed until they came to take me to the airfield. I was wheeled outside in a wheelchair and loaded onto a stretcher. Just before they slid me in the back of an Army ambulance, Dr. Miller appeared at my side. He put his hand on my arm and said, "I just wanted to say goodbye and wish you well."

I put my finger over the hole in my tracheotomy tube and whispered, "Thanks, Doc," and gave him a big grin.

The ambulance carried me to the airfield and out on the flight line to a waiting C-141 cargo plane. It had been fitted with stretcher holders lined up against the walls and down the center. Two burly men carried me on a stretcher to the center of the big cargo bay and connected my stretcher to one of the middle posts.

Ahead of the area where the stretchers hung were six rows of airline seats, I was hoping they would let me ride in a seat. A nurse came up to my stretcher and offered an extra blanket. When I asked if there was any chance I could ride in a seat, she informed me it was against the rules. She said I had to stay on the stretcher until we got to California. She told me she would be checking on me from time to time during the flight.

The plane was beginning to fill up now. The number of incapacitated men being shipped back to the States surprised me. We were all stacked into the plane like carcasses of beef. It seemed we were merely cargo, loaded on for the non-stop flight from Japan to California. Once again, I was reminded of the cattlelike existence of infantrymen.

The flight was long and arduous. It was very uncomfortable lying on the stretcher for the entire flight. But I was finally going home! It seemed like a very long time since I had been home. I had learned to bear the pain and I knew this pain would soon pass.

I nodded off near the end of the flight and was awakened by the pilot's voice over the intercom, "We're currently off the coast of Northern California and will be landing at Travis Air Force Base in about twenty minutes."

A weak round of cheers went up from the men on stretchers. I was nervous and excited at the same time.

Chapter 10

The Cruelest Blow

The huge cargo jet made a glass-smooth landing at Travis AFB in Oakland, California. I could hardly contain my excitement. I was *really* back in the United States and I was home from the war! I didn't think I would feel this elated over homecoming, but I was suddenly very excited about being back on my home turf.

It was here I was dealt the cruelest blow of my entire ordeal. When the plane came to a stop on the side of the runway, a big truck backed up to its large rear cargo doors. The truck was equipped with racks to hold the stretchers. Two big, burly guys got out of the cab and started loading the wounded up the ramp onto the back of the truck.

As they carried my stretcher to the truck, I tried to reach down and touch the ground with my good arm. I just wanted to touch the ground as a symbol of being back on American soil. I was *so* glad to be back home I wanted to feel some sense of grounding myself in the United States. I wanted to celebrate my homecoming. Even though Oakland wasn't exactly home, it was close enough for me! I pleaded with the men carrying my stretcher to lower me to the ground and they coldly refused. I was devastated by their indifference and insensitivity. I wanted to celebrate my return home, but the burly stretcher-bearers dashed my hopes.

I had hoped there would be people here to welcome us home. I believed our homecoming was important, but it appeared the only ones who felt that way were those of us being off-loaded from the plane. The Spirit was sustaining me, but it hurt to be treated so routinely.

I was aware that the war was not popular. Still I thought there would be someone waiting to welcome us home and talk to us. Instead, we were taken to a loading dock at the back of the hospital and placed into an empty freight elevator.

It seemed as though they were trying to "sneak" us into the hospital. I wondered why we didn't go through the front door or the emergency entrance, like anyone else. We were proud to be back home, but no one seemed to be proud to have us back home. It hurt. I wanted to cry, but I wasn't going to give in to my emotion.

No Heroes and No Parades

Once the big plane was unloaded, the hospital orderlies quietly moved me to a separate room. No one welcomed us home. No one even smiled at us. The unspoken message I heard was, "Big deal, you did *nothing*, you are *nothing* and you don't deserve to be treated special."

There was no fanfare, no hoopla, no banner, *nothing*. I thought coming home from this hard fought war would make me a hero, at least in the eyes of other military people. I thought they of all people would understand what it was like to put your life on the line in service to your country. I thought they would appreciate those of us who had sacrificed ourselves for the war effort.

I was wrong.

The Unfairness

The two-bed hospital room was bright, clean and simply appointed. It was a big improvement over the makeshift hospitals in Vietnam and the large medical ward in Japan. As I made myself comfortable in my new bed, a pleasant-looking, uniformed nurse came in and began to take my vital signs. She was quiet and businesslike, saying very little and appearing to be totally unconcerned about my injuries or how I got them.

She started taking a brief history concerning allergies to medications, then asked to look at my wounds. In silence, she changed my dressings, administered my medications and then she left. I felt as though I was nothing more than a piece of meat to be tended by the medical staff.

It was as if my service, survival and tremendous physical ordeal were meaningless. There had been nothing to prepare me for re-entry back into life in the States. I was not ready for the stark indifference I was encountering. There was no warning —just raw, naked apathy.

It was very odd. I had survived the unsurvivable, but now I was just another casualty in a long line of casualties. There was no place I belonged. I had an underlying feeling I would be more at home in Vietnam than I was here. In fact, there was an underlying feeling of connectedness with the war zone, a connection that would be with me for the rest of my life.

I was not the same person I had been a year ago and I knew it. And I wasn't the hero I supposed I would be after fighting a war. I wasn't even welcomed back home. To this day, I am still pained by the fact no one cared enough to simply say, "Welcome home, boys!"

It was hard to be back home, in a hospital and on a ward with non-combatants. In the hospitals in Vietnam and Japan, I was treated with respect and the medical personnel understood I had survived against all odds.

The guy in the bed across from me was in a full body cast. After the nurse left, he used an electric button to raise his bed so he could turn his head and see me. He looked like the Frankenstein monster, his fully casted body lying stiffly in the bed. He could barely move, just enough to turn his head and speak to me. "What the hell happened to you?" he asked.

I motioned I was unable to speak and wrote him a little note that briefly said, "I got shot in Vietnam." Then I wrote him another note asking, "What the hell happened to you?"

He told me, "I was chasing a woman and she pushed me down two flights of stairs."

Although I never knew his name, I learned his story was true. He had been chasing after a woman who didn't want his affections and when he got near the stairwell, she stepped aside and gave him a shove. He fell down two flights of stairs and broke half the bones in his body.

I thought, "How unfair! He's been chasing women while I've been fighting a war." It was disheartening. Here we were in the same hospital, receiving the exact same treatment.

A Family's Welcome

My family made the four hundred mile trip up from Southern California to the hospital at Travis Air Force Base to visit me as soon as they heard I had arrived. I could hardly wait for their arrival. I was sure that my family would be very glad to see me and finally, we could celebrate my homecoming together.

I was in a wheelchair, sitting in the TV room when they came. I was not prepared for my family's response and they were not prepared for what they would see.

My mom came in first. I could see that "Oh My God!" look on her face as she moved tentatively toward me. She wanted to hug me but was afraid to touch me. I looked so fragile, she was afraid she might hurt me if she hugged me. She finally gave me a gentle hug as the rest of the family came through the door, but her fear of touching me was obvious.

My dad and siblings became very quiet and stared at me. I was accustomed to my appearance, but they were shocked by it. I realized I had left home a strong, healthy, teenage boy and returned a war-hardened, gaunt, skinny, battered old man. I am not sure what my family saw in my eyes; it was *not* the look of the innocent young boy whom they had known one year earlier.

From their point of view, I looked pathetic. I had lost a considerable amount of weight during my ten months in Vietnam. I had lost over sixty pounds so when my family saw me, it was a shock for them to see their wounded son and brother. I'd never been skinny in my life. Now I was emaciated. I'd played football in high school and I was a big kid. Even as a young kid, I was chubby.

Instead of being delighted to see me, my family appeared distraught. It was a very somber time and very little was said. My mom pushed me around in the wheelchair and sobbed. She looked like hell for she had almost died in the process, too. My mom told me on the day I was wounded, she had a premonition something terrible had happened. She told one of the neighbors, "There's something wrong with Billy...he's been hurt."

A few days later she got a telegram. The telegram contained devastating news. Briefly, it said, "The Secretary of the Army has asked me to inform you that your son was wounded in action in Vietnam on 17 April 1969 while on a military mission when a hostile force was encountered. He received wounds to his left shoulder, neck with laryngeal disruption and to his right eye with surgical enucleation of the right eye."

It contained no other details of my condition. A week later she received another telegram which read, "Additional information received states that the condition of your son remains the same. Period of further hospitalization is undetermined at this time."

The telegrams continued to come but were devoid of any meaty detail. One stated I had been moved to Camp Drake in Japan. Another talked of my malaria and yet another mentioned the infections. Most just indicated my condition remained the same without telling exactly what my condition might be. Understandably, my family went through a hellish time of waiting and wondering if I would ever come home alive.

My mom said she was extremely distraught over my being injured and not being able to get any definitive answers about my condition. She became quite ill and was near death herself. She told me that her friends from church prayed for both of us every day.

The ward nurse gave me permission to go off base with my family to get some lunch. We went to a family restaurant near the motel where they were staying. Of course, I had a burger and fries.

When we returned, I checked in with the nurse. She told me I would be transferred to another hospital in the morning.

Guardian Nurse

The next morning I was transferred from Travis Air Force Base in Oakland, to Fort Ord Army Hospital near Monterey, which was a little nearer to my actual home in Orange County. My family made the short trip south and found a place to stay near Fort Ord.

I had gone full circle. I was inducted into the Army and completed my basic training at Fort Ord and now, after a very long journey, I was back. I was eighteen years old when I first came to Fort Ord. Now I was nineteen, going on forty.

There was goodness and love in my heart, but my head was still full of war. Seeing my family and trying to reintegrate with them was difficult. I no longer felt like I belonged to that family, but I wasn't sure what family I felt I belonged to. My Spirit was doing battle with my mind. I desperately wanted to find a place where I could be the person I had become and still be the person I was before I joined the Army.

I wanted to believe I could go to war and then resume the life I had before I left. There was an uneasiness that stirred deep inside me. I had no idea the scars of war ran much deeper than the scars on my flesh.

The Fort Ord Army Hospital was built to treat soldiers returning from the Pacific during World War II. The main hospital was a double row of single-story, whitewashed wooden buildings connected down the center by a long corridor. They had added on to it over the years, turning it into a maze of buildings and hallways. There was a feeling of comfort in these old buildings. I'm sure it had been a healing place for thousands of soldiers before me.

My family came to Fort Ord to spend the day with me. It was good to see them, but I was glad when they left and went back home. I was tired from pretending to be a son and brother to them. I was elated to see them, but I couldn't feel the emotional closeness I wanted to feel.

The following day I got another surprise visit. Shelly, the girl I had kissed the night before leaving to go to Vietnam, had convinced her parents to make the eight-hour drive up to Fort Ord so she could visit me.

We had been corresponding while I was in Vietnam and I knew she still had a crush on me. She often said she missed me in her letters and professed her love in a shy, teenage way. My letters to her were very generic since the same letter was being sent to everyone. I hadn't encouraged her love, nor had I discouraged it.

I was very impressed she was able to get her parents, who didn't particularly like me, to bring her all the way up there to see me. She was only able to visit about an hour before they drove back home again. When she left, I was feeling overwhelmed with all the activity of the past few days and wanted to get some rest.

I had been placed on a ward with only two other Vietnam returnees. The rest of the patients were trainees recovering from minor injuries, but it turned out to be a good experience. What made it good was a nurse who took a special interest in the Vietnam vets on the ward. I think she may have served as a nurse in Vietnam herself.

She was a tall, slender woman, with long, willowy legs and beautiful ebony skin. She always looked perfectly groomed in her crisp white nurse's uniform and she exuded an air of confidence that was very reassuring.

I remember she outranked me. I was a lowly enlisted man and she was a captain, but she treated me and the other war vets with very special care. She had a level of compassion only a warrior could appreciate. I called her my "guardian nurse."

When my family came to Fort Ord after I was transferred from Travis, my father brought me a violin case and put it by my bedside. It had a bottle of brandy in it.

One night as I sat up in bed having a little taste of brandy, my guardian nurse came over and said, "What are you doing?"

I said, "Oh, I'm just sitting here playing my violin!"

She looked at me quizzically and asked, "Do you really play the violin?"

I said, "No!" I opened the case so she could see the bottle.

She smiled and kindly said, "Oh, I see."

I'm sure she could smell the liquor on my breath, but she never said another word about it.

I had been practicing covering the hole in my tracheotomy tube and talking. I had learned how to put my fingers over the hole and make small, whisper-like sounds. I wrote notes and whispered responses to the questions from my guardian nurse as we chatted together. She asked me what unit I served with in Vietnam and wanted to know how I got my wounds.

I very briefly told her about the bomb blast and the gunshot wounds, but I wasn't sure I should tell her about the out-of-body experience or the White Light.

My guardian nurse said, "You are a very lucky young man."

I told her, "The Spirit is watching over me."

She smiled in a knowing way, then told me that if I ever needed anything, or if I was ever uncomfortable, to let her know. She said she'd make sure I got whatever I needed.

A Short Flight Home

A week after my family left, the other Vietnam vets left the ward and went home. I still hadn't been to my home, 300 miles south in Santa Ana, and I was beginning to feel lonely. I'd been gone for nearly a year. I had been through hell and I just wanted to go home where I could be in familiar surroundings.

I was frustrated. I kept asking when I would get to go home. The answer was always the same – soon. I just wanted to go home where it was safe and where I didn't have to be a soldier anymore. I wanted to normalize.

The Spirit continued to motivate me. I wanted to heal and function as normally as I possibly could. My attitude was that of a nineteen-year-old. I wanted to have fun. I desperately wanted to go home and return to the life I'd left behind when I joined the Army. But my body was severely beaten and battered and it no longer functioned as a nineteen-year-old body.

It would take many months before I fully realized I could never go back to the life I had before my military service. When I went to Vietnam, I lost my youth and my innocence. Though I didn't know it at the time, I would never get them back.

I continued to tell the medical staff I wanted to go home and they continued to tell me, "Well, you'll get a pass soon."

I decided I wasn't waiting for "soon"–I was making "soon." I got myself up out of bed, put on my uniform as best I could, caught a cab to the airport, bought a plane ticket, got on an airplane and flew home.

I called my dad and asked him to come pick me up at the airport. He was surprised to hear from me and even more surprised I was at the airport. I told him they had given me leave and I was going to be home for a few days.

I spent the time visiting with family and friends. Although I hadn't told anyone I was going to be home, the word got out fast and many people dropped by to see me.

I was home for about two days before the hospital commander called.

My mom answered the phone and I heard her saying "Yes. Yes. I see." She turned to me and said, "Billy, I think you'd better talk to this man."

I could only whisper and I said a weak, "Hello?"

The hospital commander asked, "Bill, do you think it's time to come back?"

I turned red in the face and whispered, "Yes, I'll be back as soon as I can."

It hadn't taken them long to track me down once they realized I was A.W.O.L. (Absent With Out Leave). They must have figured I wouldn't return without some prodding.

My father took me to the airport, put me on a plane and sent me back to the hospital. Two MPs met me at the Monterey airport and escorted me back to Fort Ord.

They took me directly to the hospital commander's office. The commander said, "Bill, you were A.W.O.L." He shook his head and said, "I know you didn't get a chance to go home and I know it's been a long and difficult time for you. I'm not going to press any charges against you. I should, but I'm not going to. If you behave yourself, I think we can make things a little more comfortable for you around here." He saw me give a sigh of relief and said, " In the future, if you want to go home you can put in for a pass. Your doctor has assured me you will be given an extended leave once your medical condition warrants that."

I didn't say another word. I snapped off a crisp salute and walked back to the ward.

When I returned to the ward, my guardian nurse said, "Come with me."

Instead of walking me back to my old bed, she led me to a large porch off the back of the ward that had been converted into a room. She smiled and said, "This is your new bed."

This was wonderful. This would allow me to have my own space. The room had a refrigerator, a stereo and a television set! It was everything I needed to be comfortable. It was like having my own apartment.

My guardian nurse stood in the door smiling as I eagerly inspected the room. I turned to her with a questioning look on my face. Before I could speak she said, "We can't have our combat veterans sleeping on the same ward with trainees."

I realized the reason I didn't get in trouble for going AWOL and the reason I was getting to stay in this special room was because she had intervened. She was too humble to take credit for these things, but I knew it was all her doing.

As she turned to walk away she looked back at me with a sly grin and said, "Don't play your violin too loudly. You might disturb the other patients."

The next week I was given a pass to go home for the weekend. The hospital commander came to me and warned, "Forty-eight hours, that's it, Bill! After forty-eight hours, you must come back!"

My leave was wonderful. I met with friends and went to the sunny Southern California beaches. We had a barbeque at home and my father managed to stay reasonably sober through most of the day. Shelly was at my side the whole time, and although I didn't pay much attention to her, she was happy just to be near. It was all very tiring and by the end of my forty-eight hours, I was glad to be back at the hospital.

Although the trip home was pleasant, there was a feeling of discomfort. I felt like I didn't fit in with my friends anymore. A big part of my personality had changed. Psychologically, there was a part of me that did not make it home from the war. There was a feeling of emptiness in the pit of my stomach that couldn't be filled. I didn't sleep much, but when I did, it was only for a few hours and I would wake-up sweaty and anxious. I couldn't remember any dreams or nightmares, but there was a distinct sense of terror each time I awoke.

Time in the hospital seemed to fly by very quickly. I didn't make any strong connections with the doctors, but they seemed to be convinced there was little else that they could do to improve my condition.

My guardian nurse gave me a lot of attention every day and encouraged me to stay active, practice talking and focus on healing from my wounds, both physically and spiritually. She would sometimes come in and read to me or watch TV with me. Her presence always made me feel stronger. She often told me how strong I was to have survived the war injuries and let me know she thought I was a special person. Throughout my time at Ft. Ord Army Hospital my guardian nurse never breached her nursing boundaries, but there was always an unspoken intimacy between us, for which I am forever grateful.

I continued to go home on leave almost every weekend, but I always felt more at home when I returned to the hospital. My little hospital room was comfortable and I was treated with respect by the nursing staff. The Army was my home now. I was no longer at ease with the life I had left behind when I enlisted.

Discharge

One day while I was sitting in my room listening to music, a young lieutenant came in and said he was from the Judge

Advocate General's office and was going to represent me in my medical board proceedings. He was a very unassuming young man with a mild manner. His sandy blond hair stood out in wisps along the edge of his hat. Like most of the officers around the hospital he wore a dress uniform and I could tell by the paucity of medals on his chest he had never been anywhere near a combat zone.

This youthful attorney spent over an hour asking me questions about my injuries, taking copious notes on every word I was able to squeeze out and every note I wrote. Then, without ceremony, he got up and left my room. Two days later, he came back and said he was going to take me to see some doctors.

My guardian nurse helped me into a wheelchair although I was fully able to get up and walk without any assistance. The lieutenant pushed me to the far end of the hospital through a set of double doors and into a conference room.

I sat in the wheelchair in front of a panel of officers, mostly majors and lieutenant colonels. They all had medical insignia on their collars, so I guessed they were all doctors, although I had never seen any of them before. The young lieutenant stood and addressed the panel, telling my story in a dry, legal manner.

When he was finished, the officers all looked at each other, nodded, shuffled papers for a minute and then dismissed the lieutenant and me.

As he pushed me back to my room, the lieutenant leaned forward and said, "I think it went well."

I was flabbergasted. I didn't even understand what had just happened and he said it went well. I jotted a quick note on the pad I carried in my pocket and asked, "What went well?"

The lieutenant leaned forward again and said, "Your medical board."

I just nodded agreement and let it go. I didn't see the lieutenant again for three weeks. When he came bustling into my little piece of Army heaven, he had a big grin on his face. He looked directly at me for the first time since we met and announced, "You have been approved for medical discharge. The Army is going to give you a full medical retirement."

I sat there dumbfounded as I tried to comprehend what the lieutenant had just said. I was nineteen years old and he was telling me the Army was going to give me a full retirement. I should have been elated, but with all I had been through, I felt rejected. I was a good soldier and had served my country well. The Army had become a comfortable place for me and now, after less than eighteen months, they were turning me out. The lieutenant explained that as soon as my discharge was official, I would be transferred to the VA hospital in Los Angeles.

On September 17th 1969, exactly one year, six months and three days after I was inducted, the U.S. Army discharged me with a full medical retirement and all the benefits that go with it. I packed all my belongings and the Army shipped them to my parents' home.

My guardian nurse gave me a big hug and told me she would miss me. When an orderly tried to get me into a wheelchair to take me to the waiting taxi that would drive me to the airport, I refused. I told him I would walk.

He said it was against hospital policy to let me walk out.

My guardian nurse stepped in and said, "It's all right, let him walk." She told the orderly she would walk out with me.

We walked silently. I wanted to tell her how much I appreciated all she had done for me, especially for her kindness and caring. Before getting in the cab I turned to her to speak, but she quieted me with her look. She softly said. "You are a very brave man."

As the cab driver opened the door for me, she gave me another hug. When the taxi pulled away from the curb, I looked back and saw my guardian nurse gently waving goodbye.

I sadly waved back, with a tear in my eye.

Chapter 11

A New Beginning

The trip home allowed me time to think about my short Army career. I joined the Army at age eighteen and before my nineteenth birthday, I had become a hardened combat soldier. I had experienced war to the fullest. I had an out-of-body experience and traveled to another dimension of existence where I was greeted by, and communicated with, angels. I experienced extreme physical trauma that should have ended my life.

Now, still two full months from my twentieth birthday, I had a full retirement from the United States Army. In the last two years, I had more intensely experienced life, and death, than most people experience in their entire lifetime.

In a few days I would report to the VA hospital to continue my physical recovery from the devastating injuries. The Spirit was still with me, giving me guidance and helping me to find peace in my soul. The magnitude of the near-death experience had not yet become fully apparent to me. The power of the Spirit was not yet fully developed in my young mind.

This was the beginning of an entirely new life for me. I missed the Army and I missed being a combat soldier. I didn't think I would miss Vietnam and all the hardships of being a warrior, but I longed for the camaraderie and power of being in combat. Where else but in war can a teenager, or anyone for that matter, experience so many extremes of life in such a short time or wield the power of life and death so readily?

I stayed close to home for the few days before reporting to the VA hospital. Shelly came by several times to see me. We were getting closer and more intimate; a serious relationship was quickly developing. I was thrilled that someone would want to love me as a disabled person.

I thought my dreams of marriage and family were over. The idea that a woman would want to be with a man whose body was so badly damaged was foreign to me. I felt ugly. My face still badly deformed, an empty right eye socket deeply sunken and a steel tube protruding from my neck did not make for a handsome appearance. I could only speak in whispers and it was painful to say more than a few words. I had deep, ugly scars on my face, neck, chest and left arm. All of this did not paint a picture of an attractive man. I was grateful that Shelly loved me and wanted to pursue an intimate relationship.

Shelly drove me to the VA hospital in Los Angeles. After I checked in I was directed to go to the fourth floor where I would be assigned a bed. Shelly kissed me goodbye in the lobby and I went up to the fourth floor on my own.

The ward was a large, open bay with twelve beds lining the walls. A large, bleached blond nurse greeted me. She said, "You must be William."

I nodded.

She showed me to a bed in the corner of the ward. She explained I would be responsible for keeping my bed and the area around it neat and clean. She said there would be a linen cart on the ward twice a week and I would be responsible for changing my bed linens when the cart arrived.

This place felt uncomfortable. I didn't mind making my own bed but I had a gut feeling that the quality of care was not up to the standards of the military hospitals where I had previously been a patient.

The nurse made me put on pajamas and a robe. She put my clothes and valuables in the narrow metal locker next to my bed. After she took my vitals, she told me the doctor would see me later.

When she left, I crawled under the sparse covers and took a nap.

Consent for Life

The doctors at the VA hospital probed me, poked me and finally determined that I needed an operation on my throat. They scheduled me for an exploratory surgery to determine if there was a way to repair my throat so I could breathe better. I still struggled to breathe through the tracheotomy tube sticking out of my neck.

On my third day at the VA hospital, one of the doctors took me into his office and said, "Uh, I need your mother's telephone number."

I asked, "Why?"

The doctor replied, "Because she has to come and sign a consent form for us to do the surgery." The doctor told me I needed my mother's consent to have an operation because I was only nineteen years old, not yet of legal age of consent. It was so unbelievable to me.

The irony of the situation was difficult to reconcile. When I joined the Army, I didn't need my mother's consent. Once in the Army, I "belonged" to them and I didn't have any rights. They could do anything they wanted. I was government property. They could perform surgery on me and they didn't need anybody's consent. But now that I was in the VA hospital as a civilian, they needed my mother's permission. My country would let me die for their freedom, but they had to have my mother's permission to improve the quality of my life!

It seemed that now that I was a civilian there were many things I was not allowed to do without a parent's permission or until I became of age. I was still too young to get married, too young to drink, too young to vote, but not too young to have repeatedly risked my life for my country and the "freedom" that was so casually enjoyed by the adult population in this country.

The incongruence between my spiritual being and my material being was becoming more acute. It was just the beginning of a long and difficult reintegration into civilian life.

The surgery went well but the doctors determined that very little could be done to improve my breathing. They told me I would have to have a tracheotomy tube in my neck for the rest of my life. I was disappointed by their decision to cease any further efforts to repair my throat and I knew they were wrong.

The Strength of the Spirit

Even though I had many discouraging and painful experiences, the Spirit remained strong. The Spirit from the same bright Light in my near-death experience carried me through the difficult times. I rarely felt concerned about my wounds. I rarely felt worried about the outcome of surgeries. I was confident my wounds would heal and I almost never felt "bad" for what had happened to me.

The only time I ever felt "bad" about what had happened was when other people expressed their own discomfort about it or when they pitied me. It seemed to affect them so much more than it did me. I didn't want others to suffer for my pain. To me, it was a normal part of my life.

The Spirit instilled in me a sense of peace that overcame all of the pain and concerns about my physical being. I certainly felt the pain, but it was just a reminder I was a living, breathing and functioning human being.

Initially the Light was so powerful and the Spiritual presence was so intense I didn't think much about the evilness of the war. I was just glad to be home.

Even though it was nearly twenty years before I heard the term "near-death experience," what I knew about this experience was that it made me feel positive and hopeful about life. I instinctively knew the Spirit was an incredible life-giving force. What I didn't know was how many physical and psychological obstacles would threaten the reality of my hopefulness.

Adjusting to civilian life was very painful on many levels. When I returned to my old neighborhood, my friends were spooked by my appearance. Many of them were hesitant to talk to me or be around me.

Physically, I looked like hell. I was skinny, with many of my injuries still healing and my body using every bit of energy left to repair itself. My face was crushed in - I hadn't had any plastic surgery yet. My eye socket was empty, held open by a clear plastic retainer. All in all, I suppose it was a pretty frightening sight. When my friends and family were unable to readily adjust to my physical appearance, it compounded my sense of displacement and isolation.

Instant Membership

Being a disabled person is the only minority group where a person gains membership overnight. I went from being a physically healthy, rugged, fit nineteen-year-old to a person who couldn't speak or breathe without the aid of prosthetic devices.

Now I was a person who was physically *unable* to compete with "normal" people. It was difficult to adjust to the internal vision of myself which didn't "feel" disabled. In my mind's eye, I was still a healthy, young man.

Stripped of Power

As a civilian, I lost all of my power, authority and ability to take command of situations. As a combat solider, I had a tremendous amount of power and control over the lives of other people, including the godlike power to end the life of another human being. Carrying a loaded weapon into combat and having the authority to exercise the force of the United States Army instills a sense of being almighty.

As a disabled civilian, I was stripped of this power. It was a tremendous blow to my ego. I believed the Spirit had adequately prepared me for the relentless physical ordeal of rehabilitation, but I was not prepared for the emotional distress that accompanied my reintegration into civilian life.

It was extremely painful to relinquish the power and status I had as a soldier. I believed I would be able to carry that power into civilian life and exercise it as freely as I had in the military. I was sorely disappointed.

As a nearly twenty-year-old civilian, I was constantly reminded of my status as a minor. I was not old enough to buy a beer, vote or get married. Nor was I old enough to command the respect I had previously known as a combat soldier. It was a terribly confusing time. Although, in the midst of this difficult transition, the Spirit gave me hope that all would be well if I invested my energies in my physical recovery. I knew this would help me adjust emotionally as well. I trusted the Spirit would eventually lead me through to a very fulfilling life.

A Grim Prognosis

Throughout my rehabilitation, the doctors continued to paint a very grim, despairing prognosis for me. I was told I would need permanent tubes in my throat and I would never be able to speak again or breathe properly. I was told I would completely lose the use of my left arm and it would be better to amputate it. I was also told my face would be badly disfigured.

I didn't pay much attention to what the doctors were telling me. The glow from the Light and the guidance from the Spirit were so intense and so complete that I responded to the constant negative prognosis with, "They just don't know what they're talking about. They're wrong. Everything is going to be okay." The negativity I experienced paled in comparison to the all-encompassing peace and sense of well-being and fulfillment I experienced within the spiritual Light.

The Light energy allowed me to be unconcerned with any of the hopeless predictions about permanent disabilities, limitations and impediments that seemed to be the principle focus of the doctors and nurses who were caring for me. The Spirit allowed me to know, beyond a shadow of a doubt, the outcome would be far different than the predictions being made.

I underwent four surgeries to reconstruct my face. I had two more surgeries to repair the extensive damage to my left arm and chest. I had to lobby strongly to keep the doctors from amputating my left arm. I never doubted I would regain the use of that arm or that I would be able to speak again. The Spirit was such an incredible, life-giving energy inside of me that I trusted the inner feeling that insisted I would recover and return to a normal lifestyle.

Going Home To Die

As I was told repeatedly, no one believed I would ever speak again or breathe without the assistance of a permanent tracheotomy tube in my neck. After ten months of being hospitalized, I grew very tired of medical pessimism and the doctors who wanted to keep me permanently hospitalized. I was ready to leave the hospital and to live without constant medical care.

No one else was ready for me to leave, but I wanted to go home and get on with my life. The doctors believed I would never be able to breathe properly without a tracheotomy tube. I had news for them. I had been practicing! I would place a cork into my tube and practice breathing. Over a few months time, I had taught myself to breathe without the tube.

My doctor came to me and told me he was going to schedule a surgical procedure to install a more permanent version of the tracheotomy tube. He said it was simple procedure and would not take long, but was necessary to improve my breathing.

I had had enough. The next morning I approached the doctor in his office and scribbled a note asking, "What will happen if I take this tube out of my throat?"

He looked up at me from his cushy chair and replied, "You'll die."

I smiled, pulled the tube out of my neck, laid it on his desk and scribbled another quick note that read, "Goodbye. I'm going home to die!" Before he could respond, I turned and walked out of his office.

The doctor was stunned and sat there in disbelief. I'm sure he thought I would pass out long before I got out the front door of the hospital and a nurse or security person would bring me back to the ward.

Within a few minutes, I was out the front door and not even breathing hard. I had studied how the tissue in the throat heals and knew the hole in my neck would close-up quickly and heal neatly as long as I kept it clean.

I eventually went back to the VA hospital to get plastic surgery on my face and to get an artificial eye. Improving my appearance was important to me. The stares I got from people when I went out in public were disconcerting. I felt sorry for people who couldn't cope with my appearance, but I knew in our society appearances were important. I never went back to the doctor who was treating me for my throat and neck injuries and he never made contact with me.

Trying to Normalize

After leaving the hospital, I wanted to normalize. I wanted to pursue the American Dream. I asked Shelly to marry me, and she said yes. I probably shouldn't have been surprised, but I still had a difficult time imagining anyone would want to spend his or her life with a person who was so severely disabled. We lived in Southern California and there seemed to be a social standard that didn't include anyone who was less than perfect, at least from my perception. In addition, Vietnam vets were not held in high esteem. Being called a baby killer (among other such slurs) did nothing to boost my ego strength.

Of course, when Shelly and I went to get a marriage license, I had to have a note from my mother because I was just twenty years old and still not of legal age. I was angry that I had to abide by these silly rules. I had taken human lives in the name of freedom, but I had no freedom. I was not yet old enough to be free. I wasn't old enough to buy a bottle of champagne to celebrate my engagement. It seemed so unfair. Any man with an earlier date of birth, regardless of his level of maturity or experience, had all the wonderful freedoms this country had to offer. But I was denied because of my age.

In June of 1970, Shelly and I were married. I thought marriage and starting my own family would make life perfect, just like in the movies. I also believed getting married would help me to leave the war behind. I was having thoughts about the horrors of combat almost daily. It was difficult, but I tried to push those thoughts out of my mind. I didn't want to think about all the terrible things that had happened while I was in the war zone.

A Voice from the Past

Shelly and I had rented an apartment and moved most of our things in, but had agreed we wouldn't live there until we were husband and wife. I was staying at my parents' house and on the morning of our wedding, as I was getting dressed in my tux, I heard the phone ring. I thought it was probably someone from the wedding party or a friend calling to wish me well. My mom called out, "Billy, it's for you."

When I answered I was shocked when I heard the voice on the other end. "Hey, Bill, it's Hank."

I couldn't believe my ears. I had often thought about John and Hank since leaving Vietnam, but never really expected to hear from them again.

We talked for nearly an hour before I said I had to go or I would be late for my wedding, Hank told me he and John had both been wounded and discharged from the Army. He said their wounds were minor compared to mine, but were enough to keep them out of the Army. He said he had tried to find John for many months and was unable to locate him. He knew John had survived his wounds and made it back home, but hadn't heard from him since seeing him leave Vietnam.

I was elated to hear from Hank and to know he and John were alive and back home. When I hung up the phone, I realized I was sweating profusely and thoughts of the war were racing through my mind. I pushed the uncomfortable thoughts from my head, finished dressing and raced to the church so I wouldn't be late.

Post Wedding Bell Blues

After our nuptials, Shelly and I went to San Luis Obispo in Northern California for our honeymoon. I had been feeling physically exhausted during the marriage ceremony and I attributed it to wedding-day anxiety. We drove the six hours north and by the time we arrived, I was feeling worse than when we had left. I was running a high fever. I assumed I had a case of the flu. We had planned to stay five days in San Luis Obispo but by the second day, I was so sick I could barely get out of bed. I finally asked Shelly to drive me back home so I could see a doctor.

When we got back home and saw the doctor, he informed me I had malaria. Wonderful! I had no idea that malaria could recur. It seemed as if there was no escape from the ravages of the war. I had been home nearly a year, but it seemed like I was continuously being dragged back to the war. I was still a warrior. No matter how hard I tried to leave the war behind and become a normal civilian, the war kept coming back to me; in my thoughts, dreams and, now, in my physical body. It felt as if the war was never-ending and there was no way to ever return home.

We went to the VA hospital to get treatment. They wanted to keep me as an inpatient for a couple weeks. Shelly was devastated. We had only been married three days and I was being taken away from her. She convinced the doctor to allow me to come home so she could care for me.

I spent the next two weeks on the couch recovering from malaria. I was delirious with fever and I wasn't sure I wanted to live through the pain again. Shelly stayed by my side and cared for me throughout the entire ordeal.

In my delirious state, I experienced terrible nightmares about the war. My body hurt so bad I thought death would be a welcome event. With Shelly's care and the medication the VA doctors had given us, I survived the battle with malaria, although it was another reminder that I was not the same young man who so proudly marched off to war.

Good Vibrations

I had now mastered breathing on my own although any physical exertion brought on a shortness of breath. Walk up a simple incline or climb a flight of stairs and I would struggle to get enough air through my narrow airway. It would often take me several minutes to recover from what should have been a normal, inconsequential activity.

My next task was to learn how to speak again. Of course, no one actually believed I would ever speak again. But I knew I would. Not because of my own abilities but because the Spirit had shown me that, indeed, I would speak again. I knew this endeavor was up to me though, as I no longer had a speech therapist. I persisted with my own regimen. I practiced day in and day out. I spent hours in front of a mirror and in my car, driving around singing to tunes on the radio.

Eventually, I taught myself how to vibrate the scar tissue in my throat to produce audible sounds. It was a painstakingly slow process because it took years to perfect tones, inflections and volume. For many years, the only sound that came out was a hoarse monotone or nothing more than an exaggerated whisper. It was several years before I was confident I could communicate effectively with others.

Even today, with my raspy voice, I cannot speak loudly or compete with other voices or noises in a crowded room. I often have trouble communicating on the phone and I have a heck of a time being understood by that silly clown at the drive-up window of the local hamburger joint.

During this period of rehabilitation, I was guided by the Spirit to seek new ways to communicate. The Spirit directed me to make the best of the abilities I had and to let go of the abilities I had lost. This gave me an incredibly positive outlook, but there were still many around me who kept reminding me of my limitations and did their best to steal my positive attitude. I was still not sure how to make use of my Spiritual direction, those little instructions that the Spirit would send my way when I needed them.

Describing The Indescribable

During the first couple of years after I returned from Viet Nam, the actual experience of the war seemed very far away. The battle between the evil of the war and the wonder of the Light was just beginning inside me. It would be many years before the true lessons of the Spirit and the Light would become clear and, in the mean time, the war took its lingering toll.

I knew instinctively I had to heal and rehabilitate myself before I could pursue my Spiritual path. As a young man, I was impatient; I wanted it all to be totally apparent right now. I tried very hard to communicate what had happened in the Light, but few people had ever heard of such experiences and even fewer believed them. No one wanted to listen to my incredible story about leaving my human body behind and entering the Spiritual dimension.

Part of the problem in communicating this Spiritual experience with others was my inability to speak well, but the greater difficulty came when I tried to describe what I had seen and experienced in the Light. I had no words to adequately convey the experience. When I was able to articulate the idea of the Spirit, people didn't want to hear about it. They didn't want to listen because they thought it was an insane notion. I couldn't understand why people didn't want to hear what I had to say about the afterlife. I began to think there was something wrong with my mind for believing in this experience.

Some said, "Oh, you just got hit in the head—you were just seeing stars." Most people dismissed my life-changing experience as an injury-induced hallucination. Others scoffed, "That's just a bunch of baloney. Nobody talks to angels, goes to heaven, sees God or talks to their dead grandfather. That stuff doesn't really happen."

It was during this time I began to doubt my experience. I wondered if I was losing my mind. Deep inside I knew what I had experienced was true, but consciously, in the light of the social response I was getting from my story, I began to have doubts.

An Internal Tug of War

The discrepancy inside between the devastating effects of the war and the sustenance of the Spirit was growing increasingly painful. I had visions of wondrous things I could accomplish and achieve and I truly felt limitless. However, I was surrounded by people who wanted to impose their social values and their limitations on me. Those social values and limitations didn't fit with the spiritual message I wanted to embrace. I wanted to talk freely about the Spirit, to say what I wanted to say, to be who I wanted to be.

Getting an Education

When I left high school, I had no desire to ever step foot in a classroom again. I was young, healthy and ready to meet life head-on. I was not a good student and I thought college would be no different than high school, that I would be constantly told I was not living up to my potential. I had no idea what my potential was, much less how to live up to it. In retrospect, I think my high school teachers let me down. They failed to challenge my potential.

After my experiences in Vietnam, I had matured well beyond my years. I now understood I would need an education to fulfill my higher purpose and live the quality of life I wanted. The Spirit was also directing me to go to college and open my mind to new experiences and concepts.

Shelly was very supportive of my return to school and improving myself academically, but there was a lot of negativity from others around me. My academic advisors, the Veterans Administration Vocational Rehabilitation counselors and several other of my "support people" didn't believe I could overcome my physical disabilities.

Since I could barely speak, I couldn't verbally counter the negativity. In turn, I was barraged with *their* limitations, *their* fears, *their* despair and *their* hopelessness. It was the beginning of a dark journey in my life. From my perspective, my circle of support began to disintegrate.

Despite the disbelief and pessimism of others, I enrolled in a local community college. At first I was treated as though I were 100% disabled, physically and mentally. As a student, my professors did not take me seriously. Instead, I was patronized as though to say, "Let's just indulge this helpless, disabled person...his education will never amount to much anyway."

I wanted to become a psychologist. I was told by the psychology professor, "You could never become a psychologist. You can't speak, you didn't do well in high school, and you'll never make it through the many years of college it takes to become a psychologist."

I thought, "What does that matter? I can do anything I put my mind to." But I couldn't speak well enough to tell this professor she was wrong. My head rang from her advice that I "should prepare to find a career where I could use my hands" since I couldn't speak normally. I was told I should seek a career in auto mechanics because it was something I had done as a hobby and I was good at it.

I didn't want a career in auto mechanics. I wanted to work with people, not machines! With this advice, there was even less room to speak about the near-death experience. It was impossible to try to describe to others what I knew and what I wanted to do with my life and why I wanted to work with people. I wasn't able to convince them I had a special gift to share with people and that the Spirit would help me to overcome the barriers I would face.

I had visions of academic achievements, of having a certain career path, of having a future and a life. I was constantly met with, "You can't do that because of your injuries, because you're not a good student, because you can't speak, etc." It seemed I was surrounded by dozens of people who were so overwhelmed by what I looked like and what I had been through, it was impossible for them to see anything other than what their *own* response would be to such a situation.

Interestingly, I excelled in academics and extra-curricular activities. I served in leadership positions on campus including being elected President of the Associated Men Students as a write-in candidate. (I have to be the only person ever elected who was unable to give a speech!) I received many awards and scholarships given by my peers and through faculty nominations. I was even given an honorary membership to the Associated Women Students!

The achievements and accolades were a new experience for me as I had maintained a very low profile in high school and had not done well academically. The new successes and appointments were truly benefits of paying attention to the Spirit, if only from a more quiet and internal perspective. I had stopped trying to talk to people about my near-death experience and focused on living my life with the Spirit hidden from others, deep inside me.

Regardless of what professors and advisors said, I knew I would rise above the disabilities. I knew one day I would speak again. I knew I would be totally functional again. The thought of being "totally disabled" never even crossed my mind.

A Connection

Since returning from Vietnam, I hadn't made an emotional connection with anyone except Shelly. We had friends but there was never much depth to those friendships. While I was going to Santa Ana College, I met Jerry and his wife, Eva. Jerry had served in the Marine Corps during Vietnam and had been stationed not far from where my unit had worked. We had been in some of the same villages and our service time had overlapped a little. I was immediately comfortable with Jerry and our wives became best friends.

Jerry and I talked a lot about the war. We could share war stories and had a certain understanding about the events of combat only another vet can fully comprehend. Although we were close and I shared stories about the war I hadn't shared with anyone else, I didn't talk to him about my journey to the spiritual dimension.

Shelly and I saw Jerry and Eva several times a week. We became as close as family and even went on vacations together. My friendship with Jerry and Eva was one of the high points of my life.

After we graduated from Santa Ana College, Jerry was accepted at Kansas State University to study architecture. He and Eva moved to Kansas that summer. I felt a deep sense of loss when they left. I was again reminded of all the losses in the military. My emotional walls became a little thicker that summer. It would be a long time before I let anyone get close again.

Spiritual Drive With No Vehicle

I had an incredible spiritual drive inside but had no vehicle to express it. Instead, I channeled this spiritual energy into other things such as forming clubs on campus and serving in leadership positions–things I had never done before. But over time, I became increasingly frustrated with the clash of spiritual values with what I considered very careless values of other people my own age.

I couldn't understand how others could be so selfish, thoughtless or hateful. I couldn't understand why I couldn't find people who shared the same values I held. I was pained and confused to believe I had been given this wonderful experience and had no way to communicate or share it.

War Protests

The war in Vietnam was still raging as I went to school. Throughout my college career, I was confronted with war protesters. Although most of the students I associated with knew I was disabled, they did not know how I had become disabled or that I had served in Vietnam. I found myself angry with those who protested the war because most of the students protesting were afraid to serve their country. They complained bitterly that we were violating the civil rights of the Vietnamese people and committing murder and killing babies.

My view of the war was vastly different. I didn't understand those who had no sense of duty or passion to serve their country. They wanted the freedom that was borne from combat but were unwilling to do what it took to earn that freedom. Worse yet, they were unwilling to respect those who had honorably served their country.

There have always been many ways to serve our country without going to war, but most of the protesters I encountered were more interested in self-indulgence and self-preservation than in discussing the real issues pertinent to the war in Vietnam. I was deeply bothered that Democracy had become such a cheap, valueless freedom that many perceived as not worth defending around the world. I agreed there was a strong secondary agenda to the war, but the primary objective was to aid the South Vietnamese people in securing a democratic society and prevent the spread of oppressive politics that silenced dissenters.

I had placed my life on the line to protect the rights and freedoms of Americans so they could speak freely and rightfully protest our intervention in Vietnam. I expected them to pay their dues as well and I expected them to respect those that served to protect their freedom. I was not a baby killer or murderer. I was a soldier, a warrior who ultimately fought for peace and freedom. What angered me most was that the protestors forced the closure of classrooms to hold their rallies. I had more than earned the right to attend classes and get a quality education and these protestors took that right from me.

Irrevocably Changed

I now realized the immense impact the Vietnam experience had imposed on me. I was radically changed. I was different from my peers, irrevocably different. I had life experiences far beyond my years and well beyond my non-veteran peers. I had the wisdom of a forty-year-old with the developmental needs of a twenty-year-old. I knew things about life and death most people would never experience or be able to comprehend until very late in life. I knew things about the resiliency of the human body and the darkness of human nature. I was not the same person I had been before the war—not physically, emotionally, psychologically or spiritually. I struggled to integrate the knowledge and experiences of war with civilian life, with the obstacles of rehabilitation and with the public rejection of the Spirit within me.

Violent Indifference

One of the greatest struggles and painful realities I had to endure was the total lack of recognition and respect veterans received upon return from military service. There were no welcome home banners, no parades, no fanfare and no thanks. No one asked any questions. No one cared. Not my caregivers (with the exception of my guardian nurse), not my family, friends, peers, colleagues and, surprisingly, not even the military!

There were no formal ceremonies to bring any type of closure to this violent experience. There were no debriefing camps to teach me how to re-enter civilian life or how to compensate for the incredible chunk of life that had been ripped away from me. The pain of indifference and utter disregard for veterans of this unpopular war made it feel as though the snipers were shooting at me again, and again, and again.

No one cared I had risked my life every single day in the combat zone or that I had witnessed vicious battles and vulgarities of suffering and pain that defied verbal expression. No one cared I was full of sorrow and grief for the countless comrades, both friend and foe, I had watched die on the battlefield. No one cared I had served with my whole heart and soul for a purpose I believed was honorable to defend.

Chapter 12

Empty Success

I was twenty-three years old and had finished my AA degree in auto mechanics, just as others had prescribed for me, without understanding what the spiritual cost would be. I was not satisfied with this level of education and went on to a university seeking a bachelor's degree.

Shelly was very supportive of my efforts to better myself and continue my education. We had a good relationship, but still did not share the same level of spirituality, nor did we discuss our spiritual differences.

The summer before I started at California State University, we purchased our first home and wanted to start a family. This put some undo stress on me since I would now have to work more hours while attending school. Shelly also worked and it was our plan that I would finish my degree and then she could return to school and finish her education. She had completed her AA degree about the same time as I had.

My voice, although very coarse sounding, was improving. I was able to communicate with significantly less effort. My practicing was paying-off. I was gaining confidence in my ability to speak out and communicate more openly.

I had gained additional use of my left arm. Through practice and exercise, I had regained about eighty percent use. I was slowly overcoming the disabling conditions doctors had told me would prevent me from living a normal life.

I was pursuing the path prescribed by my academic advisors. It wasn't the path I would have chosen on my own, but I believed that these people, with their advanced academic degrees, must know what they were talking about. I thought I should trust their knowledge and wisdom.

The Spirit had instilled in me a drive to seek physical normalcy, but I was lost when it came to my academic direction. It would take many years before the Spirit would give me a clearer picture of where I needed to apply myself academically.

What is especially interesting about this period in my life is that the farther down this "prescribed" path I went, the more lost I became as a person. From all outward appearances I was succeeding. I had a home and a wife and all the trappings of a middle class American. I could see I was where I wanted to be, but I had no feeling of satisfaction for my accomplishments.

I was physically in pain everyday. My wounds had healed on the surface, but the damage done to my body was permanent. It was difficult to breathe. I was able to speak better, but any speech was painful. Prolonged speech, such as an evening with friends, resulted in a very sore throat and a day of extreme discomfort. I wanted so desperately to be normal again. I knew I would never be a normal person, but I had hoped I could find a level of functioning that would allow me to fit in to an average, middle class lifestyle.

After a couple of years at the university, Shelly began to complain. She wanted to quit work and start a family. She said it was taking too long for me to complete my bachelor's degree. She wanted me to quit school and get a full-time job. I was only one semester from completing my degree and one year from getting my teaching credential. I wanted to continue, but I was not getting good grades and I was struggling to maintain my marriage and stay focused on my studies.

Although up to this point I had always gotten good grades, I had never been a good student. For the most part, academics came easy to me. I never put forth much effort studying or reading the textbooks. I was able to quickly grasp the concepts presented in class and apply them to practical application. This method of learning worked well most of the time, but there were situations where this method failed me or could not be readily applied.

Due to the poor quality of my voice, I failed the speech test that was ultimately necessary to get a teaching credential. This was a situation over which I had no control. After much explaining about what had happened to my vocal cords and insisting I would get better with time, I was able to get my professor to give me a waiver on the speech test.

Asking for special consideration took something out of me. I now knew no matter how hard I tried I would always be a disabled person. The Spirit could give me the drive to be normal, but it could do very little to completely overcome the physical damage I had sustained. I realized talking to a classroom full of noisy students everyday was going to be painful and exhausting. I could see my choice to pursue a career as a teacher was probably not a wise one. It seemed all I had worked so hard to accomplish was going for naught.

Feeling defeated by my inability to achieve my goal of becoming a teacher, I gave in to Shelly's complaints, quit school and got a job as an assistant manager in a retail auto parts store. I quickly advanced to a management position. Even though my body functioned poorly, my mind was sharp and I worked hard.

Once I was established in the work force, Shelly promptly quit her job and became pregnant (although not entirely on her own). We were elated, but a few months later, she had a miscarriage. We were very disappointed, but the doctor said there was no reason we couldn't try again.

Six months later Shelly was again pregnant and again she miscarried within a few months. Shelly and I were both devastated by this turn of events. I was depressed and was reminded of all the battlefield losses. I had nightmares again and the war was on my mind frequently.

The Vietnam War had ended in defeat several years earlier and Vietnam vets had been branded as losers. I was beginning to feel like a loser. The only place I could escape my feelings of despair was at work.

I changed companies every six to eight months in an effort to make more money and get a better position. I advanced from one management position to the next, but the harder I strived to be a good manager and a good husband, the more empty I felt inside.

In my struggle with middle class life, I knew something was terribly wrong, but I didn't equate it with being on the wrong spiritual path. I continued to believe that something was intrinsically wrong with me. As a material being, I was still trying to find language for my Spiritual encounter. Adding to my despair, when I tried to tell others about this magical out-of-body experience, I was quickly assessed as a lunatic. I couldn't talk about the war and I certainly couldn't tell anyone about my journey to the Spiritual dimension.

It was a difficult concept for me to grasp. To have risked my life for my country and then to be treated with such disdain and violent indifference was incongruent with my ideals and experience. It was this discrepancy that caused the internal conflict within me to escalate and consume me. I became increasingly angry and frustrated with life.

Remarkably, I still had enough spark in me I didn't want to just give up on life. I still tried to enjoy life, to work hard and to accomplish new things. I still wanted to work with people. Since I "couldn't" be a psychologist, I dreamed of opening a retail business. I wanted a hobby and craft store, but I needed the support of my wife. Shelly was unable to share my vision and refused to support this endeavor. She insisted if I were to open a retail business it had to be in auto mechanics because that was where I had some expertise.

So, I opened an automotive shop. It was a successful endeavor, but I never liked it. It wasn't my vision, it wasn't my dream and it wasn't on my spiritual path.

Shortly after I opened my automotive shop, Shelly announced she was, once again, pregnant. The pregnancy went smoothly this time and we were blessed with a beautiful baby boy. We named him William VandenBush IV after my grandfather, my father and myself. I was very proud to have a son. Prior to his birth, my relationship with Shelly was strained. I hoped this wonderful child would improve our relationship and draw us closer together.

Having a baby in the house was great. He was a good baby and a joy to care for. I thought my dream of having a middle class family and lifestyle was coming true. But having a child put pressure on me to earn more money. I worked longer hours to keep my business profitable. My long hours and the pressure to raise a family and keep my wife happy became overwhelming. Within a year after William was born, my marriage to Shelly deteriorated to the point we decided to get divorced.

I was crushed; my dream had turned to a nightmare. I had always believed that marriage was a lifelong commitment and you didn't give up on that kind of commitment. Shelly believed there was no choice. She was unhappy I was spending so much time at work while she was stuck at home caring for the baby.

She was convinced there was no way to reconcile. We had grown so far apart in our desires and ideals there was no way to find our way back to the love we once shared.

It was a very sad and confusing time for me. I wanted to be with my wife and child and live the American Dream. Shelly wanted us to be making more money and living a higher style of life. She also thought we should be emotionally closer than we were.

I was showing signs of Post-Traumatic Stress, although I had no idea what it was at the time. Depression, irritability, emotional detachment, constant nightmares and, when I wasn't focused on my work, I had memories of the war running through my head constantly.

Earlier in our marriage, I had experienced periods of anger and rage. Although I had never harmed Shelly, I had instilled a fear in her that made her believe I could one day lose my temper and hurt her or young William. My anger had cooled since that earlier period, but the emotional damage to our relationship had already been done.

Shelly and I were not emotionally mature enough to sit down and have a heart-to-heart talk. She left and took my precious son with her. We went through a bitter divorce and I was plunged into the depths of despair. Shelly's mother had been terribly abused by her first husband who was a disabled veteran. She believed I was going to eventually abuse Shelly and my beloved child. She supported Shelly in her efforts to divorce me and went to extreme efforts to help Shelly separate our lives and keep my son from me.

I may have been an angry Vietnam vet, but I was never physically abusive to any human being. After the trauma of war I couldn't bring myself to harm human or animal. I certainly knew if my life, or the life of a loved one were threatened, I was very capable of using deadly force, but the thought of doing harm to anyone or anything was sickening to me.

I often withdrew from social situations. I hadn't realized it at the time, but the only people I had allowed myself to be close to were other Vietnam veterans. I attributed my social shyness to my inability to communicate effectively and my physical disfigurement. The scars on my face and neck and my raspy voice were far more obvious to me than they were to others, but then, I had to look at myself and my disfiguring scars in the mirror everyday.

My divorce forced me to sell the automotive shop and when the divorce was final, I had nothing to show for the last ten years of hard work. My house was gone, most of my belongings were gone, my son was gone and I was unemployed. My dreams had been shattered. Shelly and her mother had cleaned me out, materially, emotionally, and even my Spirit had grown weaker.

A Dimming of the Light

Little by little, the Spirit within me began to fade. Eventually, I gave up on the Spirit. I gave up trying to find others who shared the same spiritual values I had come to embrace. I began to believe I must be "wrong" because everywhere I turned there was so much negativity.

With each tempest of negativity, a little piece of the Light inside of me was extinguished. Eventually, I was overcome by the negativity. The Light that was once a beacon of hope was now nothing more than a glimmering pinpoint in the depths of my heart.

It was as though all the goals this inner driving spiritual force attempted to guide me toward were thwarted by the negativity of others and my own self-doubts. I was losing the strength to be myself and find myself in that spirituality.

As the faith drained out of me, my life started to turn away from the sustenance of the Spirit and the guidance from the Light. I didn't become an evil or bad person; I just became a lost soul. I felt completely and totally lost.

A Journey Into Darkness

My life was in shambles. I felt devoid of the Light and was losing the last sense of well-being and completeness I had known before. I became increasingly more depressed as I faced the negative side of life. It was a terribly dark and hopeless time.

I began to have terrible nightmares. I was a mess. I was devastated by my divorce, the loss of contact with my son and the loss of my business, but this merely served as an appetizer to the darkest period of my life.

For several years after my divorce, I was held captive by the negativity until finally the Spirit was silent within me. My drive was gone. I felt tired, weak and disabled.

In retrospect, I believe this was a testing of my faith and belief system. At the time, however, I didn't understand because I was met with so much opposition. So, I turned to the one area I could rely on for self-esteem: employment.

After a long search, I found a job with the Environmental Engineering Division of a large corporation. This company did a wide variety of environmental testing on automobiles. I was able to apply the automotive skills I had developed.

I started as a test technician and within six months I rose to a management position. I enjoyed my work and the people I worked with, but I was experiencing a deeper emptiness than I had ever known.

The money was good and I attempted to buy my happiness and fill the spiritual void with material possessions and toys. I was purchasing my life piecemeal. When I was feeling unfulfilled, I would go spend money. The material objects gave me pleasure, but that pleasure was always short-lived.

Since material objects weren't giving me any lasting fulfillment, I thought I should find a mate and remarry, hoping to rekindle the feelings of love and spiritual fulfillment I had when Shelly and I first married.

I met a woman named Pat. She had gone through a messy divorce and was as much on the rebound as I was. I don't think we ever considered that we were not in love. We were madly in *lust* and that was enough. We were each filling the emptiness that exists when a long-term relationship ends. We never stopped to completely examine our emotions and motives. The warmth and closeness of our bodies gave us something to cling to, a life-ring floating in the debris of a sinking ship.

Two weeks after we found each other, we drove to Las Vegas and got married. As we stood at the altar, we were both keenly aware this was *not* the right thing to be doing, but it was a lark. We said our vows in the emotionless assembly line of the Vegas wedding chapel, then proceeded to honeymoon with gusto in one of the many bridal suites in a swank hotel on the strip.

Within a few months, the lust had tarnished and the marriage was on the rocks. We mutually agreed to divorce and went our separate ways. The spiritual emptiness was now greater than ever.

Chapter 13

A Place of Renewal

In 1980, the company I was working for transferred me to Seattle, Washington. From the moment I arrived, I knew Washington would be a special place for me. The tiny speck of Light in my heart flickered briefly. I worked long hours as we founded a new corporation and developed a contractual relationship with Washington State Department of Ecology.

We implemented an automotive emission-testing program in Seattle. I thought this program had value and significance. I was proud to be part of the team. It reminded me of the teamwork necessary to carry out our missions in Vietnam.

I invested myself heavily into my work in an effort to block any thoughts of the war and the emotional pain I suffered. Physically I had to cope with the challenges of living in a world full of "normal" people and compete with those physically "normal" people for jobs, promotions and raises. It took all of my energy to compete on the job and when I was done working for the day, I had to rest.

While others enjoyed a social life after work, I was always too tired. I had only enough energy to do my job well; there was nothing left for extracurricular activities. I worked hard and the project came together smoother than I imagined it would. Opening day was flawless and all the work that went into preparing the project paid-off handsomely.

Within a few months, work was going well and I was in line for another promotion. I felt connected to the company and thought I was on the right career path. Then came a big surprise, I was laid-off.

My initial thought was, "This is no big deal. I have some money in the bank and I know I can get work before the money runs out." I was offered a job in California, but I didn't want to go back. Washington felt like home now. There was a sense the Spirit was alive here and I couldn't bring myself to leave.

I took a little vacation to clear my head before beginning my job search and, as soon as I returned, I hit the pavement in search of just the right position to maintain my lifestyle. I was sure it wouldn't take long to find a good job. After all, I had years of experience and a hat full of confidence.

I searched and searched, but everywhere I turned, there were no jobs for me. I had come from California where the cost of living was higher and the pay scale was much higher than in Washington. My experience and earning level were too high for the area. I would have to lower my standards if I were to get hired in the Seattle area.

I asked for less money, offered to take entry level positions regardless of pay and still no one would hire me. I applied for jobs for which I knew I was well qualified and continuously got turned down.

I was depressed and became Spiritless during this time. My life sank to a dismal level and I contemplated whether it was even worthwhile to continue living. I was devastated by my impotence in finding gainful employment.

My search for employment lasted over six months, until I became so depressed I quit going out on job interviews. Piece by piece, I watched my life disintegrate before me. The money I had saved quickly ran out. I had to sell my car, relinquish all of my possessions and move to a shack of an apartment. Eventually, I lost everything.

Divorced, unemployed, penniless and alone, the darkness continued to consume me. I believed my life was in a rapid downward spiral. I felt powerless to change it. I had frightful mood swings and isolated myself from social situations.

I didn't want to go to bed at night because I was having terrible nightmares about the war. I was irritable and full of rage. I felt out of control. I couldn't seem to make anything work in my life. I couldn't find any reason to continue living.

I recalled the last time I really loved life; I was in the Light and full of the Spirit. Dying seemed like the only pathway back to the Light. What I didn't know was that I was experiencing the same symptoms that would later be termed "Post Vietnam Syndrome" or PTSD (Post Traumatic Stress Disorder) by the mental health community.

A Knock At The Door

As the despair over my situation deepened, my mood darkened and I began to slip into a deep depression. I withdrew further into myself and continued to stay isolated in my apartment. I was extremely confused by the turn of events in my life. No matter what happened in my personal life, I'd always been able to rely on my professional life to get me through tough times. Being laid-off from my job and not finding another to take its place was the last straw for me. It was as though someone had taken the oars away from my rowboat of life, and now I was careening out of control, heading straight for Niagara Falls.

I was helpless, and hopeless to "make life happen" on any level. I felt shrouded in a fog of darkness. I had lost my ability to navigate out of this pit that was suffocating me. I seriously contemplated suicide. The actual thought of killing myself terrified me because it violated all I had learned from the Spirit. The message from the Spirit was life was to be lived all the way to the natural end. The difficult times were as much a part of life as the good times. The difficult times were not just to be endured, but were there to teach us something about ourselves.

Still, I sought relief from the pain and darkness that enveloped me. I wanted another encounter with the Light to renew my Spirit and clarify the Spiritual lessons.

One day, while sitting alone in my barren apartment contemplating whether to live or die, there was a knock at the door. The very last thing I wanted was company. I hardly had the energy to answer the door. But the knock persisted and drew me to see who was there.

I pulled myself off the couch and answered the door. Of all people, it was the AVON lady. I'm not sure why I let her in, but I did. It didn't take her long to surmise that I was broke, desperately depressed and very much alone.

She stopped trying to sell me "Avon for Men" and rambled on about the singles group at her church. As she talked about her church and finding hope through Christ, I thought, "I've got to get rid of this woman!"

Then she started telling me about an upcoming retreat with the single's group. I thought, "There's no way I'm going to a church retreat." There was no way I was going to be around a bunch of "Jesus freaks" who would try to rescue me with their religious ideals. What I *wanted* was to be left alone. What I *needed* was to be rescued from the cliff of despair.

When she mentioned the cost of the retreat was $60, I thought, "Aha, my ticket out! I can't afford a quart of milk, much less sixty bucks for a retreat!"

I protested, and politely declined her offer stating, "I'm sorry, I can't afford the sixty dollar fee. Maybe next year when I'm in a better place financially."

It didn't work. She told me that she and her husband provided scholarships for people who couldn't afford the retreat. She was relentless in her campaign and eventually I gave in. I reluctantly agreed to go to the retreat, but I couldn't really figure out how this was going to help.

A Flicker Of Light

Paradoxically, it was during this extremely dark time that I caught a flash of the Light again. Although I had grave reservations about going to the church retreat, something inside me said, "You need to do this. Attendance is non-negotiable; there is something you need to learn." The Spirit was speaking to me and I knew instinctively I needed to listen.

On the day I was to go on the retreat, I reluctantly went down to the church and found a seat on the bus. I didn't know anyone, so I sat alone and quietly looked out the window.

As we drove through the countryside, a little of the fog in my outlook began to lift. I realized that since I'd moved to Washington State, I had never really taken the time to look at the scenery. I began to notice the immense beauty that surrounded me. There were lush green trees, majestic, snow-capped mountains and deep blue bodies of water everywhere.

Washington was a virtual paradise compared to the barren stretch of southern California where I was born and raised. I was struck with the depth of beauty all around me and I was seeing it for the first time even though it had always been there.

The retreat site was in a secluded location up in the mountains. The bus drov up a long, twisty dirt road to reach it. When we arrived, there were half a dozen log cabins surrounding a main lodge. The lodge housed the kitchen, dining hall and a large meeting room. The meeting room was very inviting with an oversized, rock-lined fireplace. The view from the lodge was a picture-perfect setting of woodlands and meadows.

I was struck by the strange sense of peace and warmth I felt in this place. It was good to be in touch with Mother Nature. I collected my gear and settled into a bunk in one of the cabins. I took advantage of the free time in the schedule before dinner to relax and enjoy the scenery.

After dinner I mingled with the other guests in the meeting room. I was warmly received and chatted for about an hour. It had been several weeks since I had real contact with other people. It felt pleasant. I was starting to relax a bit and felt glad I had decided to attend this retreat. I was very tired and decided to turn in early. I went back to my bunk and quickly fell asleep.

The next morning I awoke feeling well rested and full of energy. I couldn't remember the last time I'd felt so refreshed and full of life. I took a walk in the fresh, cool, morning air.

The retreat site seemed even more beautiful and serene than I remembered it from the day before. The air seemed crisper; the trees were taller and greener; the meadows appeared even were more lush and beautiful than before. The air smelled and tasted fresh and clean. I noticed the edges of the branches on the trees and the way the breeze hypnotized the meadows in their movement. The thick cloud of distortion in my head was beginning to fade.

I walked through the woods to a small meadow and sat down on a fallen log. It was so peaceful and calm; I felt a million miles away from civilization. In the stillness of the morning, I felt the presence of the Spirit from the Light well up inside of me. I felt the indescribable peace and unconditional love I had known in the Light, returning to me. A sense of awe filled me. In front of me, a family of deer emerged from the woods and began grazing in the meadow.

A Bolt of Lightening: Simplicity

Suddenly, something dawned on me. I thought about the sheer beauty and simplicity of nature and realized the deer instinctively grazed in the meadow. They accepted and respected each other. They shared the sunlight, the water and the meadow together. Simply. Without complications or difficulties. That was it! Simplicity was the key to life. It wasn't the accumulation of material possessions, wealth or position that would bring peace, love and contentment in my life. It was simplicity. Now I understood. A life of simplicity, not suicide, was the way back to the Light.

At that moment, I knew that I needed to return to the values of the Light and to follow my Spirit, trusting I would be guided to positive, fruitful things in life just as the deer were instinctively led to the meadows to graze. I began to feel the Light and the Spirit's glow inside of me again.

As the wonderful things I had learned in the Light began to return, the feeling of unconditional love overwhelmed me. The fluidity and comfort of thought returned, the universal knowledge of life returned and the beauty of life returned to me in that one beautiful moment.

It was as if a bolt of lightening had hit me and I was suddenly reborn into a world I had once known well. I was no longer adrift in a foreign sea.

I sat on that log until the Light and Spirit grew still inside me and faded into a small, burning ember deep in my soul. At that point, I became aware that no matter what happened in my life, the Spirit would be there. It was clear the road of life would continue to be rocky and my human drives and influences would occasionally drive me off the Spiritual path.

Now I knew regardless of how far I might stray from my higher purpose, the Spirit would always be there. I became fully aware that the Spirit always exists within us.

There is no process by which we access the Spirit, it is always there and we need only step into the Light through our desire to do so. Unfortunately, the nature of being human, and social, sometimes causes us to forget the strength of our Spirit and how to access that strength.

No longer fearful of losing the Spirit, I knew I had the power to turn that ember into a raging inferno to guide me to the earthly knowledge I needed to fulfill my higher purpose in this dimension of life. For the first time in many, many years I felt peaceful and fulfilled. I knew my dark days were over and that, in time, the Light and the Spirit would once again fill me with joy, desire and the direction I needed to restore my faith in the power of the Spirit.

I spent the next two days enjoying the beauty of the natural surroundings and literally drinking in the marrow of a life restored. I chatted easily with others and felt a sense of belonging.

During the lectures on spirituality, I was able to make the connection between the Spirit inside of me and the one the others sought so hard to find. I began to understand this Spirit was common to all people, not just Christians, but people of all faiths. The Spirit inside me was a universal force and it was guided from another dimension of existence. The Spirit was eternally connected to the Light and to me.

Now I understood the importance of attending the retreat! The retreat was merely a catalyst for a reconnection with the Spirit. For the first time in a very long time, I believed people cared about me and my life mattered. I began to realize that reconnecting with the Light and the Spirit was the essential element that had been missing from my life.

When I returned home from the retreat, my mind raced with tasks I needed to get busy doing. My impulse was to rush right out and start "making life happen" again.

As the Spirit began to grow intense in me, I felt a sharp warning to "slow down and simply let life happen." Instead of trying to take control of everything, I understood I had to allow life to come to me. I needed to let go of the control so I could clearly see the options in order to follow the path to my special purpose on Earth.

I was puzzled by the familiarity of the admonition. I had known this from another time in my life...but when? Then I remembered that during the healing from my physical trauma, this same Spirit had given me the same words of encouragement: "Let go."

I instinctively knew it was time to allow the Spirit to guide me. I knew I had to trust the Spirit to teach me what I needed to learn and to take me where I needed to go. In the recent years I'd become so lost in life that finding the way on my own was an impossibility. But now, I felt fully restored to life!

Within days I no longer felt depressed or hopeless. The desire to live was stronger than I'd ever remembered. I was full of anticipation for the journey on which I was about to embark.

Chapter 14

Classroom On Planet Earth

Still unemployed, I was about to learn one of my first Spiritual lessons. As I thought about looking for work, I realized my desire to run through my usual course of career promotions to earn more money had lost its glitter. That was odd. If money wasn't my goal, then what was? I wasn't sure, but the Spirit was.

I wrestled with the question of money until the Spirit ended the match. As I listened, I was told the money wasn't important, but rather, the work was important. If I let the Spirit guide me to find work, the money would follow and I would have all the things I needed and wanted.

Additionally, I was reminded I needed to "let go" of my materialistic sense and learn to trust my spiritual sense. This encounter was one of the first things that had true meaning in nearly a year of unemployment.

Within two weeks I was offered a job as a Youth Corps Supervisor with the Washington State Department of Ecology. It was only a temporary job, but it was good work and the pay was above average.

During this temporary position, the Spirit began to come alive in me again. I was working with people and truly enjoying it. My energy levels began to increase and I realized the obstacles that had seemed insurmountable just a few weeks before were a wild deception. For the first time in years, I felt able to start fulfilling my dreams.

Back in the recesses of my mind, I still secretly dreamed of working in the field of psychology. I dared not share my dream. My earlier dream of being a psychologist had been sufficiently bludgeoned to death by others. Besides, I had no academic qualifications to become a psychologist or a counselor. Still I dreamed of becoming a counselor some day.

Privately I wondered how any of this would coincide with the initial message from the Light that had told me I had a higher purpose to fulfill. It had never been clear to me exactly what that purpose was or exactly how I would fulfill that purpose.

Around this time the Spirit began to speak to me again, in very simple terms. Not an audible voice, but rather in very simple messages through my thoughts. The thoughts were comforting, as though they were an echo from the Light. The message was straightforward: "You must talk to people. Your words will heal them, their words will heal you."

This thought, "You must talk to the people," kept ringing through my mind. I had no idea how to go about talking to the people or even which people to talk to. I knew the Spirit would take me where I needed to be if I could let go of the human desire to resist stepping into the unknown.

I didn't recognize the gift I was given by the Spirit, but it was the gift of healing. I was being prepared to reach out to touch the lives of others and improve the quality of their lives.

It was during this time that some friends encouraged me to do some volunteer work. Volunteer work? I couldn't imagine it. Me? From my current perspective, volunteering did not serve as a gauge to measure my success, fulfillment and happiness in life. I needed a paying job. I didn't really want to volunteer, but the Spirit inside urged me to go along with it. This was definitely not my usual path—volunteering didn't pay money!

Few things made sense in my life at this point, so I figured, what could this hurt? The one thing I was sure of was the Spirit was guiding me now.

"All right, I'll do it," I thought, not completely convinced. I volunteered at the Folk Life Festival in Seattle, mostly to impress a woman I was dating.

Another friend urged me to get involved with Special Olympics. I volunteered to be a Special Olympics coach and, to my surprise, I felt gratified in the work and fascinated by the people I met. I had little idea of how important the volunteer work would become.

The Perfect Job

As I continued to develop my spiritual sense about how I fit in this material world, I became more aware of the many ways the Spirit within was directing my life. One of most peculiar nudgings was through a job interview in the automotive industry.

For ten years, my career path had been in the automotive field. While I enjoyed the temporary position with Youth Corp, I continued to look for employment in the automotive field. I assumed I needed to stay in this field to earn money to return to school for the necessary education to become a counselor.

As I searched for a job, I found a job opening at an auto parts distribution cente I believed was perfect for me. Just perfect.

I applied for the position. The interview went extremely well. The employer told me, "You're the best candidate that has walked through the door. You're head and shoulders above all of the other candidates for this position. You would be perfect for this company."

I grew excited in anticipation of being offered the job. I relaxed in my chair as my mind raced toward salary negotiations.

His next words sent a shock of electricity through my body. "Bill, I'd really like to hire you, but there's just one thing. It seems to me that you're more suited for social services."

I couldn't believe my ears! I thought, "What *are* you talking about? The auto industry is my career; this is my chosen field. It's my background. It's where I have all my employment experience. This job is tailor-made for me!"

He continued, "I'd really like to hire you but I don't think you'd stay very long or be very happy in this job."

I couldn't believe what I was hearing.

Driving back home, I spent hours wracking my brain trying to recall what I might have said that caused him to make that remark. I was mystified by his insight. I couldn't think of anything I might have said that would lead him to believe I wanted, or needed, to work in the social services.

As I thought about the interview, I remembered there was something very odd about the entire situation and the way he was able to read me. It felt somewhat surrealistic.

His office was in a tiny room atop an automotive warehouse. It was very unpretentious, rather plain and ordinary. *He* was very plain and ordinary, but I had a sense I had spoken with a Higher Power. Looking back, I know he was placed in my path to help lead me to my higher purpose. I've often wondered whether he really existed or if he was just another encounter with the Light.

Mulling the conversation over and over, the puzzle pieces began to slip into place. Early in my college career, I had dreamed of becoming a psychologist, only to have my ambitions and desires squelched by others. I had thoroughly buried this dream until it resurfaced during my reconnection with the Spirit at the retreat. I thought long and hard about what the potential employer had said. Then I pondered, "Maybe I need to place some trust in this advice."

Learning to Listen to the Spirit

The encounter with the employer was not an isolated incident. I began to have similar experiences that defied explanation. Out of the blue, people both known and unknown to me made comments like, "Have you ever thought of being a counselor?" or "Gee, you have good people skills." I was both delighted and apprehensive. Becoming a counselor was the deepest desire of my heart, yet I had no clear idea how this would ever be achieved.

Around this time, I had begun my own therapy process and was involved in a "rap" group with other Vietnam veterans. I had read some articles about Vietnam Veterans who were having trouble readjusting to civilian life and were having nightmares and memories of the war that they couldn't control. The VA had set up storefront counseling centers called "Vet Centers" to help veterans who needed counseling but didn't feel comfortable going to the VA hospital for care.

I was well aware I fit the criteria for what they were calling "Post-Vietnam Syndrome." I needed some help and this seemed like the best place to get it.

I participated in this "rap" group for sixteen weeks. At the end of the four-month period, the facilitator approached me and invited me to be a co-facilitator of the next "rap" group.

I was elated! I couldn't believe my ears. Enthusiastically, I replied, "Sure, I'd really like that!" I could hardly believe I was asked to be a co-facilitator. I secretly thought, "Could this be the first step toward reaching my dream to be a counselor?"

The first night of the next session, the facilitator raced up to me with a look of panic on his face. He said, "I've got a real problem. The other facilitator quit and now I have two groups meeting at the same time. You'll have to facilitate this group on your own...can you do that?"

I said, "You bet!"

This challenge really lit a fire in me. I devoured everything I could read on group therapy and "Post-Traumatic Stress Disorder," as I had found out Post-Vietnam Syndrome was officially called. I spent every free moment learning what I could about group dynamics, group facilitation and how to become a counselor. During this time, the intensity of the Light came to grow inside of me once again. It was the guidance and drive provided by the Spirit that enabled me to devote such intense study time to this subject and to learn as rapidly as I did.

For the first time in years, I began to regain confidence in myself and the desire to become a counselor grew stronger than ever. All of these events were signs that told me I needed to change and grow and all pointed me toward this new spiritual path. I wondered if this career path toward counseling was a piece of the higher purpose, "talking to the people," that the Spirit had communicated to me.

Blinking Signals, Neon Lights and U-Turns

Up until this point, it seemed my life had been a wandering journey down a barren highway. No blinking signals, no neon lights, no exit signs. Then suddenly, all these road signs appeared in various forms; all these extraordinary encounters happened to point me back towards a spiritual path. Or perhaps, more accurately, it was the Spiritual Energy leading me back onto a spiritual path.

I began to pay more attention to these urgings, impressions and encounters as road signs for my spiritual journey. I began to grow in my awareness of my own spirituality. I began to nurture what I knew spiritually, and most importantly, I began to trust the Spirit more readily in the direction and the Way I was being led. Extremely extraordinary things began to happen within the ordinariness of life.

Ever Thought Of Being A Counselor?

My temporary job with the Youth Corps ended and I was once again frustrated in my effort to find work. I knew I needed more education if I were going to land a job in the Human Service field.

Right after my job with the Youth Corps ended I had applied for VA Voc Rehab benefits to help pay for my education on the road to becoming a counselor. I got a letter in the mail stating I'd been denied educational benefits to return to college and get a degree in Human Services.

I called the VA Vocational Rehabilitation Office; I was extremely angry and wanted to see someone about this immediately. The person on the phone said it would take several weeks to get an appointment to see a vocational counselor.

I decided to drive to the Federal building in downtown Seattle and talk to someone in person. By the time I arrived, I was really steamed and demanded to be seen by someone in authority. The clerk at the desk said the best he could do was let me see Scott, the veterans' representative from the State Employment Security Office, who was out stationed to the Voc Rehab office for the day. I begrudgingly agreed to see him.

In the course of making my complaint known, I ended up shouting, as best I could given my raspy voice, obscenities at the representative. I railed at him for several minutes about the denial of my educational benefits.

Scott was a tall, skinny redhead with an innocent-looking freckled face. He sat calmly in the tiny office and when I had exhausted myself, he replied, "Have you ever thought about being a counselor?"

I thought the guy had gone off his nut. It was as though he hadn't heard a single word I'd said. I had verbally trashed him. His reply was calm and polite. It didn't compute. I gathered my wits and responded, "Yeah, I'd like to be a counselor."

Once I calmed down, I knew this had to be a plot of the Spirit at work because it was just too bizarre for description. Things like this just didn't happen in real life.

With that, I left his office with a lead to interview for a counselor's position with Washington State Employment Security Office in downtown Seattle.

A Snowball's Chance

When I went to apply for the job, I quickly became aware of the incredible qualifications of competing applicants. The room was filled with people with graduate degrees and years of experience in the counseling field.

I thought to myself, "What on earth am I doing here? I don't have a snowball's chance in hell of getting this job. I have no experience in this field and I don't even have a bachelor's degree. All I have is an Associate of Arts degree in auto mechanics! Fat chance!"

Although convinced it would be a fruitless effort, I went ahead with the interview and, to my surprise, it went fairly well. But I didn't delude myself. On top of everything else, my speech was still somewhat impaired and so my communication skills were limited.

The next day I got a call from the Employment Security office and was offered the job.

I thought, "This is totally insane. How did I end up getting this job?"

I mustered my curiosity and asked why I was chosen for the job. I was told that while many of the other candidates were more qualified, had more experience, education, etc. I was the only applicant who had spent time volunteering while seeking employment. It was that desire to continue to work, whether the jobs were paying ones or not, that had enticed them into selecting me.

I was stunned...the volunteer work? Without the guidance of the Spirit, I probably would not have volunteered my time.

A week later I began my first paid counselor's job as a veteran's representative in the Washington State Employment Security Office in downtown Seattle. My desk was not more than four feet from Scott's, the man who had calmly listened to my tirade and offered to send me on the interview that landed me this wonderful job. Unreal.

A Dance with Faith

After about eighteen months at this dream job, the unthinkable happened. There was a scandal in the office and everyone in the department was terminated. In one quick, blanket action, the entire department was eliminated. I was in a state of shock, mystified and unemployed...again. I had done absolutely nothing wrong, yet I was fired from my job.

I began to doubt my spiritual path. If this job had arisen through a series of divine appointments, then why was it being ripped away from me? I didn't understand.

I thought, "Come on, give me a break up there!" It didn't seem right, it just didn't seem right.

Chapter 15

A Quiet Conspiracy

Two weeks later I got a call from the Seattle Vet Center where I still volunteered in my spare time. I was told about an opening at the Vet Center for an entry-level counselor's position.

I applied for the position and two days later I was hired. For anyone who knows about the difficulties of securing government positions, it was nothing short of a miracle I ended up with another government job that quickly.

By this time I was becoming accustomed to the strangeness of these situations. I once again knew this was another abrupt turn on my spiritual journey. Although I was headed in a new direction, I was confident I was still on the right path, led by the Spirit.

Although I had landed another job, I was still fighting to redeem myself with the Employment Security Department and had hired an attorney to help me get my job back. Since I had done nothing wrong, I knew I would eventually be rehired. I turned the situation over to the attorney and the Spirit so I could concentrate on my new job.

It was the job at the Vet Center that began to solidify my convictions about this spiritual path and about the desire to become a counselor. I knew I wanted to become a counselor, but I didn't quite know what kind of counselor to be. I enjoyed my work at the Employment Security Department as a vocational counselor, but I wasn't sure that was exactly where I wanted to be. After having worked through my own PTSD (post traumatic stress disorder) issues and having gone through my own therapy process, I had really enjoyed the work I had done as a volunteer with the PTSD groups. I began to think about what it would mean to work in the mental health field.

Meanwhile I knew my case with the state would come to hearing soon and my attorney assured me I would get my old job back. I enjoyed working at the Vet Center, but wanted my old job back since the pay at the Vet Center was only half of what I had made at my previous job. (No, I hadn't quite learned the lesson about letting go of the money.)

One day I received a call from a friend who said, "Hey, the VA is starting a new PTSD program at American Lake VA Hospital in Tacoma and they're hiring counselors. You'd be really good. You should go down and apply."

My initial response was, "I don't want to do that! I don't want to go to Tacoma. I live in Seattle and I like Seattle." With that, I dismissed the silly notion.

About two days later a different person said the exact same thing to me, nearly verbatim. I thought, "What gives? This smells like a conspiracy to me." Again I dismissed the idea. I had a job and I was most likely going to be reinstated in my state job.

Within two more days, two more counselors from the Vet Center approached me with the same message. Finally, Dr. Anderson, the psychologist from the PTSD treatment program where I volunteered one night a week said, "Hey, they're opening a new program…"

I thought my hair was going to catch fire. I thought, "Okay, okay, I get it, I get it. I don't need a finger from the sky to write it out for me. I just need to go to Tacoma and apply for a position in this new program they're starting"

By this time, I had to recognize and listen to the Spirit. I knew I was meant to be a counselor in the PTSD program at American Lake VA Hospital.

Listening to the Spirit again, I gained confidence in my ability to be a counselor even though I had no credentials. There was no doubt in my mind. After so many cues, I knew this was the place for me whether I wanted it or not. I knew to step away from this would be a mistake.

I picked up the phone and called the director of this new program. I told him my name, that I worked at the Seattle Vet Center as a counselor and that I would make a very good counselor in his program. He told me to come down to American Lake for an interview.

I interviewed with three people who asked me numerous and terrifically technical questions about mental health issues. Everything I knew about mental health I had read in a book. Everything I knew about working with people who were mentally ill had come in my very brief experience as a counselor at the Vet Center and through my volunteer work. Gulp. I hemmed and hawed at the questions and did my best to wade through their inquiries.

A Pop Quiz: Do The Work, The Money Will Follow

The following day, I was offered the job. The timing was perfect as the job at the Vet Center was temporary and was ending soon and I had not yet regained my job with the Employment Security Department.

The week after I finished my temporary job at the Vet Center, I began working at the VA Hospital at American Lake. Two weeks later I received a call from the Employment Security

Department. I had been exonerated of the wrongful dismissal. I was reinstated with full back pay and a request to come back to my old job.

I believed this to be a pop quiz on my spiritual path. The question of money rose to the surface again. My old job paid a much more handsome salary than what I was earning at the VA Hospital. Now I had a decision to make about which job I would choose to keep.

A lot had transpired in the recent months. I felt sure that I was to pursue a career in the mental health field. I knew the position at the Vet Center and at American Lake was a part of a grander plan. What became even more crystal clear to me was that from the moment the Light had flickered back on in my life, nothing had been random.

In fact, I began to realize nothing had been random in my life, not the decision to join the Army, my tour in Vietnam, the ordeal of being wounded or my rehabilitation. I was profoundly touched to know all these events were, in fact, part of the "higher purpose" I'd been called to. Nothing had been coincidental or chance luck. Nothing!

All of these events had a common thread to them, a common strand and a common scheme. The common thread was simplicity. I did nothing to manipulate situations, strive for opportunities or look for stepping-stones toward my dream of becoming a counselor. One of simplicity's lessons was teaching me to let go of making life happen and allow life to come to me.

As I thought about which job to choose, I remembered the earlier admonition: "The money's not important. It's the work that is important. Do the work and the money will follow."

If I returned to my old job, I knew it would be a step backwards in my spiritual journey. I began to understand the old job was merely a stepping stone, a vehicle to bring me to this point in my life. I decided to keep the job at the VA Hospital.

The admonition was correct: I received several months of back pay from the Employment Security Department which allowed me to purchase a much needed automobile to make the commute from Seattle to Tacoma. Eventually I knew I would have to give in and relocate to Tacoma.

The Roaring Fire of Awareness: Just Show Up

I'm not sure if I just became more aware of the daily blessings of life or if there was an increase in them, but it seemed as though one good thing after another happened in my life without my doing much to bring them about.

One day as I was driving to work, I noticed a tall, slender, blond woman posting a "for rent" sign in front of a duplex about a half a mile from the entrance to the VA Hospital. During my lunch break I drove out the gate and inquired about the duplex.

It was a wonderful place right on American Lake. It was loaded with extras, a spacious kitchen, laundry facilities, fireplace, all of the personal things I preferred in a home and it was more affordable than I could have ever imagined.

As I stepped inside the duplex, I felt such peace and contentment. Once again, my spiritual path was sanctioned. It was the only place I had looked at in Tacoma. I wasn't familiar with the area nor had I previous opportunities to investigate the surrounding area. The moment I stepped foot in this duplex, I knew I wanted to live there and no further search was necessary.

It occurred to me that a very large part of my spiritual path was merely to "show up" and accept what was being presented to me at the time. There was no striving and stress. This journey was becoming increasingly more simple. I learned I merely had to pay attention to what was going on around me and the opportunities would appear.

I've often wondered how many times people have missed incredible opportunities and blessings simply because they were not paying attention to life. The spiritual path is simpler than most imagine.

A Paradigm Shift

When I began my job at American Lake VA, I had no particular agenda for the job. That was a very big change in my approach to employment. My usual mode was to look for ways to advance into management as quickly as possible. I decided to stay at American Lake as long as the Spirit urged me to stay.

During my first year there I realized that to continue in the mental health field, I would need to complete more education and get some solid credentials. Remember, I only had an AA degree in Automotive Mechanics. I was thirty-seven years old and I hadn't been in a classroom in fifteen years. I wasn't sure how to go about getting my education restarted.

I still dreamed of obtaining a PhD in psychology. Remarkably, several individuals told me I would make an excellent clinical social worker. I didn't really understand any of this at first, but learned that when the same message was sent through multiple messengers, pay attention! Although I thought I wanted to be a psychologist, my Spirit was telling me to get a degree in Social Work. By this time, I had learned to listen to the Spirit and pursue the path on which I was being guided.

When I seriously considered returning to school, I became discouraged. With my past academic history, my age and years away from school, I knew I was not in line to receive scholarships or to gain entrance to a prestigious school.

When I applied to the University of Washington, I was told that very little of my previous education would transfer as usable credits and that much of my class work was simply too old and outdated to be acceptable toward a degree. Deep sigh. The prospect of starting over at thirty-seven years of age as freshman in college was incredibly daunting.

I resigned myself to the fact that it would take years to complete a simple bachelor's degree and, with that, I would still probably need to take additional social service classes at a local community college before I would even stand a chance of acceptance into a graduate level social work program.

A First Quarter Senior

I met Janet, a graduate social work intern during my first year at the VA Hospital. Janet and I became friends and she had made several attempts to urge me to get back in school.

One day while we were having lunch, I was again making excuses why I couldn't go to school right now. Janet grabbed me by the arm and said, " I want you to take the rest of the day off and come with me. You need to be a social worker." Janet was very forceful and wasn't going to take "no" for an answer.

She drove me to the admissions office of The Evergreen State College in Olympia, Washington. I thought it was all very interesting. I didn't know anything about The Evergreen State College, but later learned that it had a very prestigious reputation across the nation as a college of excellence.

During the inquiry with an admissions counselor, I learned that Evergreen would accept every last credit of my associate degree and all of the other college courses I had taken earlier in my life. They also said some of my military experience could be used for college credit.

When I left the admissions office that day, I had learned I could be accepted at The Evergreen State College as a first-quarter senior! I would only have to complete three quarters of coursework in psychology and sociology to earn a bachelors degree. I was speechless.

I immediately filled out all the necessary paperwork and within a few months was notified I was accepted at Evergreen as a first-quarter senior and I would need to complete 60 credits to obtain a Bachelor of Arts degree.

I thought, "Geez, when the Spirit guides, it takes the express lane!" I was thrilled. The only snag was I couldn't begin classes right away because I had enrolled too late for the fall quarter. I had to wait for the winter quarter to begin so I decided to enroll in a psychology class at the local community college in the meantime. Just to get back into an academic frame of mind.

Attending the community college was a wonderful experience for me. I was eager to learn and gained increasing confidence in my academic abilities. In fact, years later I wrote a recommendation for my psychology professor when he applied to teach at The Evergreen State College.

Asking and Receiving

It was so clear to me that the Spirit had guided me through the entire admissions process at Evergreen. The more I learned to let go and trust my Spirit, the simpler and more meaningful life became. When I thought I'd never be able to finish school, that I wasn't smart enough or that I couldn't manage another problem on the job, I relied on my Spirit to teach me what I needed to learn from the situation. I learned to ask, "Okay, what now? You got me this far. Where do I go from here?"

What amazed me was that the more I asked from my Spirit, the more I received. Asking and receiving are such simple truths, I am still puzzled why we trip on the simplicity of it over and over again instead of just accepting it as truth.

Whatever challenges I faced, I was supplied with the skills to overcome them. If I needed better study habits, I developed them. If I needed to assert myself, the courage came. As long as I allowed the Spirit to guide me, I was given everything I needed for whatever situation I faced.

Hatred Confronted

At Evergreen I was stretched to learn how to express my opinion even when it was a vastly unpopular one. One of the most growth-producing situations that confronted me was a radical group of individuals who voiced their open hatred for Vietnam veterans. It had been seventeen years since I'd heard the term "baby-killer." I had not felt as much animosity toward me since my return home from Vietnam. At a time when it seemed the rest of the world had finally come around to embrace Vietnam veterans, I found myself in an environment where certain people clearly had not. This was a learning curve for me.

At first I was hurt by the expressed hatred targeted at Vietnam vets. I tried to listen and understand what this group was really angry about. I couldn't believe they could really be angry with the men and women who had fought to defend their freedoms. I fought for my country to preserve our freedoms, including the right to free speech, regardless of whether or not I agreed with what others had to say.

Then I realized they blamed the veterans for the war itself. They erroneously based their views on the assumption the soldiers somehow had control over the war and thus perpetuated it. They were unable to see that the politicians had controlled the war, not the veterans. My hurt at their harsh words turned to sorrow for the way their rage devoured them and the way their inability to see the truth deceived them.

I learned to express my opinion, but I didn't argue with this group or attempt to set them straight on the facts of the war. Instead I learned I couldn't change their opinion and it wasn't my job to try. This experience was a large part of my education and I understood I needed to live my own life, follow my own path and allow others to do the same. I learned hatred is a very powerful force and people do not necessarily "grow out" of it.

The following year I graduated from The Evergreen State College with a bachelors degree. The degree earned me a promotion and an opportunity to be more challenged in my work. I continued to work at the VA and at the same time, began thinking about getting a masters degree. No sooner had I received my diploma, than Janet, who had dragged me down to enroll at The Evergreen State College, began dogging me about the Master of Social Work program at the University of Washington in Seattle.

Against All Odds

While interested, I resisted the idea of getting a masters degree because I assumed I would have to attend classes full-time during the day. I couldn't quit my job, but Janet was very persistent. Again she dragged me off to the admissions office and explained, "You can enroll in the evening program. You can attend classes at night and work during the day."

I was very skeptical. But I jumped through the hoops, filled out the paperwork and sent it off. I knew of other individuals who worked at the VA who had years of experience and background in social service and who were a lot smarter than me (so I thought) who had not been accepted to the evening program. So what chance did I have?

Months later I received my letter of acceptance to the program. I was shocked and ardently elated. When I floated back down to earth, I knew that again, divine intervention had played a role in this admission. I let go of my fears a little more and trusted that my part in all of this was to simply "show up, attend class and learn."

By this point I had learned it was easier to be led by the hand instead of being booted from behind down this spiritual path! I was deeply impacted by all of the divine intervention in my life. I didn't always want to follow the Light, but I knew better. I had been on the other side of darkness and I knew I didn't want to repeat that journey.

In Spite of Myself

Although I was accepted into the evening program at the School of Social Work at the University of Washington, it was a three-year masters degree program and I didn't really want to be in school for three years. I asked my Spirit for guidance.

In short, I was able to complete the program in a little over two years. So many of these things happened in spite of myself. Even when I said, "No," and thought I meant it, the answer seemed to be "Yes." Finding a way to finish the program in two years was a clear affirmation of this. Sure, there were times when others sought to pull me off this path, but the path had become so clear I could not allow myself to be pulled away from the Light by anyone or anything.

During graduate school I began to appreciate the uniqueness of my spiritual experience and journey. I knew about the Spirit, trusted it and had rekindled it to some degree. Once I began to nurture this Spirit, the experience I had in the Light in 1969 returned to me with the same intensity and vividness I had originally experienced. The radiance, the warmth, and the all-encompassing power of the Light filled me again.

The Light became more than a spiritual awakening, it became a way of life. The Light guided me, carried and surrounded me. Whether anyone believed my near-death experience or understood what it meant became less important to me. I knew the experience was valid regardless of what other people thought.

The continued accessibility, presence and guidance of the Spirit confirmed to me I hadn't imagined any of this. The Spirit was not a figment of my imagination, nor was it some kind of psychological phenomena. A psychological phenomenon does not guide a soul. Neither do dreams. Dreams and psychological phenomena fade with time. This Light continued to grow in its intensity. It didn't fade away. The more credence I gave to the Light, the more intense the Light became. It became increasingly clear that following the Light was the only viable way I could possibly live my life.

During graduate school I began to write papers about my life experiences, although I shied away from writing or speaking about my near-death experience. Disclosing the near-death experience posed an enormous risk to me as I was very unsure how people would react. I was only beginning to understand the full scope of this magical, life-altering experience myself.

My philosophy of life and spirituality was clearly my own and no one else's. Writing from my own experiences was not the most conventional way to write term papers, but it was my way. I often felt as if I wrote them from some other dimension. I was astonished at how effortless the exercises were for me. I had never been an academician; I had always just barely scraped by. I was even more astonished that my papers earned high marks and awesome regard from the professors. Me?

A Personal Risk

Near the end of graduate school, I still had not written anything about my near-death experience. Nor had I told anyone about it. I had not divulged how I had acquired the information I had about spirituality, or where the information came from to write my papers. I expressed my spiritual opinions as my personal observations of life.

It had been seventeen years since I talked about my near death experience to anyone and it hadn't gone so well the first time, so I was still apprehensive. The last thing a person who is about to launch a career in mental health services wants is to have his sanity questioned.

During a class called Confrontations with Dying and Living, the professor posed a question for discussion in our small groups. He asked each of us to tell about our most significant experience with death.

I winced at the question and thought, "Okay, Supreme Being, did you do this? Is this your idea?" I debated what to say. I wasn't sure if I should risk telling the story of my near-death experience on the battlefield in Vietnam.

As I quieted myself, the Spirit whispered to me, "This is the time. This is the place. Have faith. Tell someone."

I began to speak to the group and told them about being badly wounded and my experience in the Light. I could see by the expressions on my classmates' faces they were profoundly moved by what I shared. Some were, perhaps, jogged a little back on track with their own spiritual journey.

The professor overheard me telling my story and he said, "You know, what you had was a Near-Death Experience."

I had never heard the term before. I had never read anything about it nor had anyone ever framed my experience with that phraseology.

He continued, "There's a person in Seattle who's kind of an expert on Near-Death Experiences. She runs a group. You should contact her. Her name is Kimberley Clark Sharp."

Like most people, I thought, "Yeah, yeah, yeah. Everybody is full of great ideas about what I *should* do with my life."

The professor gave me her phone number and an article about the International Association for Near-Death Studies (IANDS); I took the information but had no intention of calling. I responded with my brain rather than with my Spirit.

A Small Gathering

About a year later, I had finished graduate school and was wandering through a tiny public library in Parkland. I noticed a small poster that advertised a near-death studies group that met monthly at the library. I remembered that my professor had mentioned something about "near-death." I decided to check out this meeting and see what all of the fuss was about.

I went to this small gathering and as was customary, I told my story. The first thing out of the leader's mouth was, "There's a person in Seattle that you should meet..." Sure enough, it was Kimberly Clark Sharp, the very same person the professor had mentioned to me almost a year earlier.

I thought, "Aha! I'm catching on quicker. I now only have to hear something two times before I figure out the Spirit is sending me a message. Yeah! It's only taken me a year to figure this one out!"

I made plans to attend the Seattle group gathering. When I arrived and met Kimberly, I was immediately comfortable with her. She asked me if I would share my story. It was hard for me to believe my story had any significance because, after all, it was just the story I had lived with all my life. I was still in awe of the response I got from people who heard my story.

I agreed to her request thinking it would be a small gathering. We had gotten there early and there were only a couple dozen people sitting in the room. As the meeting time neared, dozens more people arrived filling the room with nearly one hundred people!

I thought, "Yikes! I'm not sure of this!" In all these years, I had only told my story twice. I waffled about getting up in front of this crowd, but then remembered how deeply impacted people in Parkland had been when they heard my story. It was this reminder that spurred my courage to go through with it.

A Silence Broken

When I sat next to Kimberly on the stage in front of this room full of strangers, I felt a deep and familiar connection with her, as if our souls had known each other from another dimension or another time. Then I began to relax and tell my story. I took my time speaking and as the story unfolded, I could see a transformation in the eyes of those who listened. People were spellbound by what I had to say. I was amazed. When I finished, I was swamped with questions from dozens of people wanting to know more.

This was the beginning of a new era for me. I was offered a number of speaking engagements and several television appearances. After twenty years of silence, suddenly everyone was interested in what I had to say about my journey into the Spiritual dimension. The Spirit compelled me to share all I knew about this other dimension and how my near-death experience influenced my life.

I was invited to talk shows and local newspapers wrote feature articles about me. In many ways, it was all very fulfilling to be able to finally express what had been inside of me and guiding my life for so many years. Here I was, a man that was not supposed to be able to talk and had been given such a poor prognosis for survival, speaking to thousands of people about an event that no one wanted to hear about twenty years earlier.

I began to understand that something in the telling of my story had a profound impact on other people. It moved them. It changed them. It brought them closer to their own Spirit. The more times I told my story, the stronger the Spirit grew inside of me. The more the Spirit grew in me, the more my understanding of how it influenced my life deepened and the more it made the lives of others grow.

After many years of telling my story, I understood that the Spirit from the other dimension of existence had a deep and profound influence on me and could also have a deep and profound influence on the people I came in contact with. In addition I realized that it doesn't have an influence on everyone. I wondered why. Pondering this has caused me to look more deeply into the spiritual truths and lessons that I've learned along the way.

The Never-ending Story

There is no end to this story. My life continues. There have been many wonderful moments and some not so wonderful moments. I am still a human being and the battle between being human and being spiritual continues to rage within me.

It is very difficult to find the balance between the Spirit and all the incredible strength it brings to our lives and the nature of being human.

I live in pain everyday from the wounds I received in the Vietnam War, both the physical and the emotional. I worked a full time job as a clinical social worker at the VA Hospital until March 2000, when I took a medical retirement. The story of my life continues and my knowledge of the Spirit grows stronger with each passing day.

The fact I am still alive and relatively healthy is nothing short of a miracle. I owe this miracle to the Spirit and I will enjoy each day the Spirit gives me.

The Spirit has taught me many lessons over the years and I would like to share those lessons with anyone who is interested. A newspaper reporter once asked me, "How are you going to convince people that what you say is true?"

My response was, "I am not going to convince anyone of anything. I am merely sharing my experience with them and they can do with it as they please. The only person who needs to know my story is true is me and that I know without doubt.

Chapter 16

Lessons from the Spiritual Dimension

The lessons from the Spiritual Dimension are not easy to learn and this chapter may require extra attention. The spiritual lessons make more sense when read slowly and deliberately. There are no definitive terms in the English language to describe the Spirit or the spiritual dimension. I have done my best to try to explain, in simple terms, a few of the lessons I have learned from my own personal experience.

To begin with, spiritual lessons require a certain amount of faith. Once we make a connection with our own unique Spirit, we must trust, or have faith, that it will help us in our journey through life. I hope that sharing some of the lessons I have learned from the Spirit and the Light will help you to be a more Spiritual being and help you to find the Spirit that is uniquely yours. Additionally, it should be understood your unique Spirit is an integral part of an even greater universal Spirit.

Hope

Hope is the driving force that allows us to get through difficult times knowing that better times are just around the corner.

Discovering a life lived from a perspective of hope and hopefulness is one of the many rewards of a spiritual journey and spiritual path in life. Hope is a necessity for a fulfilled life, not a rare commodity. Finding hope in the midst of everyday life begins with a choice to find or rediscover our spiritual path and our spiritual self.

Ultimately, we discover that the wellspring of hope is found in the Spirit and we humbly realize it has little to do with our own human abilities. In other words, it requires no special intellect or ability to connect with our own unique Spirit. Anyone can do it.

There may be many reasons why we have distanced ourselves from a spiritual path and we may have solid evidence for why this area of our lives has become squelched or even disowned. Yet, a deep yearning, or a gnawing emptiness within, signals us back to an internal need to be on a simpler, more enlightened spiritual path.

My experience in the Light and my consequent life with the Spirit, taught me the Spirit is universal. It is a universal link between all people regardless of their spiritual beliefs, religious convictions, affiliations or status in the religious community.

When we pass from this life, we pass without the encumbrance of our body and without all of our trappings of societal values, judgments, discriminations and distortions. Spirituality is universal. When we pass from this world to the next, we take our Spirit with us, or should I say, we go where our Spirit takes us.

There are no religions in the Spirit world; all Spirits are of the same belief, but have a unique persona. In the dimension that exists beyond death, there is no discrimination between beings (no race, religion, color or nationality biases). We become beings of Light energy, but carry our own individual personality.

One of the most interesting things I learned about the Light and the presence of the Spirit is that it can come to us in the midst of ordinary, everyday life. Our Spirit can come to us as we simply live. Living by the Spirit does not mean that we isolate ourselves from the rest of the world or the rest of humanity. Instead, it is in the midst of humanity we truly learn to live and become completely, and Spiritually, fulfilled in this life.

We don't have to do anything special to connect with this Spirit that exists within each of us; there are no special rituals, no special clothes, chants, songs, or prayers that will automatically bring the Spirit to us. The power of the Spirit exists at all times and in all places. We merely have to reach out and grasp the Spirit. Accept it and it will be there for us. The Spirit is always there for us to connect with and communicate with. All that is needed is the faith that the Spirit exists.

Spiritually Connected

The first time I became fully aware that the Spirit is universal was when I was laying wounded on the battlefield. Terror and panic set in as I realized I was dying. My wounds were very serious and there was no one around to help me or any aid in sight.

As I sought to absorb the incredible reality of my impending death, I was consumed with feelings of intense loneliness. I knew that I was going to die far away from my friends, family and home. The likelihood I would die alone was imminent since the other squad members were not in close proximity to me. The loneliness I felt was compounded by feelings of injustice that I would die so young. All my hopes, dreams, and expectations for life swirled past me at the speed of light.

As soon as I accepted death, the feelings of loneliness, injustice and disappointment instantly vanished. None of my previous concerns mattered.

There was a sense that I was suddenly connected to this whole, vast universe. I felt I was an integral part of something immensely greater than myself. The temporal concerns of seeing my family, returning home and achieving the American dream had no relevance in this spiritual dimension.

Once I entered the Light, there was a universal connectedness with all beings which was all encompassing. There was a deep sense of unconditional love for all Spirit Beings and this unconditional love was a feeling shared by all of those beings within the spiritual dimension. Along with the tremendous connection, there was a sense of belonging I have never felt in any earthly social situation. Even though this was clearly a different dimension of existence from the human dimension, the spiritual connectedness is relevant to every human being as well as every spirit being.

On the earthly plane, the connection to our own unique Spirit connects us to all other human beings, as well as to the Spirit dimension. This connection is similar to the connection one feels to nature and animals, although the connection to other humans is intensely stronger. We are a part of, and have a Spiritual relationship to, all natural creations. As we begin to understand the universal nature of the Spirit, it is then logical to seek out our place and purpose in life. That search begins with a quest for balance in our lives.

Our purpose in life is to first find a balance within our human selves, within our souls and within our earthly environment. Once we have found the balance, the purpose of life is to find joy, peace, and fulfillment in our lives through service to people, Spirit and nature. It is also to find love within ourselves that we can share with others. Our fulfillment comes from our understanding, and love, for ourselves, as well as in our connections with other people and nature. In addition, it is our purpose to fully experience the human condition. This means we must find fulfillment in the pain, sadness and difficulties we experience in the course of being human.

To reach that purpose, we have to find our common connection with each other. If we can begin to understand our

Spirit, we will have a far greater chance of understanding our own humanness. If we understand our humanness, our imperfections, our weaknesses and flaws, we are then better equipped to relate to and connect with others around us.

A Personal Relationship

Although the Spirit is Universal in the sense that it is available and accessible to everyone, the Spirit is uniquely personal and individual in how it finds access and expression within each of us. Your unique Spirit can only come to you through personal reflection. It cannot be discovered or given to you by someone else.

We each have to be willing to look within ourselves to the times in our lives when we felt at peace with others and ourselves. If we take time for personal reflection, we begin to become aware of what events, elements or activities bring us peace; then we are likely to begin our awareness of the Spirit and understand how we can access the Spirit in our daily lives.

Understanding the Spirit is universal and available to all is important, but equally important is to understand the incredible accommodation the Spirit makes to us as individuals. Our part is to become aware, respond to the Spirit and develop our Spiritual path.

There is no such thing as a point of arrival in our Spiritual path. Spiritual fulfillment is dynamic, ever changing, and we, too, must be ever changing to be fulfilled.

Serving and Receiving

Part of the connection and fulfillment with the Spirit has to do with service to others. It has to do with teaching others and sharing what we have learned along the way. Once we've become aware of our own Spirit and have learned what it means to be on our own Spiritual path, then we have a responsibility to share it with others. Actually, sharing the information becomes another piece of being re-energized spiritually. The business of teaching and giving away our knowledge is very critical to our personal growth and fulfillment. Nothing given to a hungry soul is ever lost.

Many people genuinely desire to have a greater understanding of the spiritual aspect of their lives, but lack the tools to bridge the gap between desire and experience. I am often asked how to access this Spirit or Guiding Force within.

There is no process, formula or simple 1-2-3-step guide to spirituality. Our spirituality or spiritual self is available to us, anytime, anywhere and under any condition. But, our spiritual self is not born out of doing. It is born out of being. Whether a person is seeking to explore their own spirituality for the first time or seeking to reconstruct a spiritual life that has fallen into disrepair, the concept of being self-aware will be one of the most important aspects of fulfilling a spiritual life.

Self-Awareness: The Touchstone of a Spiritual Life

One of the foundational touchstones on the path of a spiritual life is self-awareness. This awareness is developed over time and it is never instantaneous.

Awareness begins with slowing your life by taking time to relax, breathe and move more deliberately. Awareness occurs in the absence of doing and in the absence of busyness. As you move more slowly, you will have time to acknowledge daily life instead of experiencing the blur of one day into the next. When you intentionally set aside time to develop awareness in your daily life, you will begin to notice the world around you and the life that happens outside of, and in spite of, yourself.

Developing daily awareness is not about moving mountains. Rather, it begins simply and slowly with something as automatic as breathing. Slow down and notice how you are breathing. Stop to feel the sensation of the breeze or rain upon your face. What direction are the trees swaying? How blue is the sky? Slowing down to notice the way that you breathe or notice the environment you live in, is among the simplest ways of developing inner awareness.

Awareness begets awareness. As you practice simple ways of experiencing daily life, you will learn that as a human being, you are intrinsically connected to all living things. The more aware you become of the simplicity of life, the more aware you will become of the complexity of life. The more aware you are of all that is around you, the closer you will get to being in-touch with your Spirit.

To begin this process of awareness, simply STOP all activity, conversation and mental plans for fifteen minutes. At first, silence and inactivity feel dull and boring. It will feel uncomfortable because it is not familiar and you may not have a lot of practice sitting quietly and observing your environment, or paying attention to the details of life around you.

To become fully self-aware, you must become aware of *all* that is around you, not just what is visible to your sight, but what is *available* to all of your senses. Once you practice, you will become accustomed to sitting quietly and being aware of all that is around you. Eventually, as you practice self-awareness, it will enable you to see what is beyond your basic senses. Self-awareness is what will enable you to develop a Spiritual sense.

As you begin to notice the richness of colors and the textures of your surroundings, you will start to see your environment from a new perspective, learning to appreciate the simple lines of your furniture, the warmth that emanates from wood grains, the depth of the color painted on your walls, the intricate design and richness of the textures of fabric you touch or lounge on.

When you slow down to gain awareness of living things outside of yourself, you will prepare yourself for a new inner awareness. It is the inner awareness that carves a path to your Spirit. When you build a path to your Spirit, the Spirit grows stronger and more apparent within you, but often there will be barriers on your path to the Spirit.

Striving toward awareness, you must be willing to remove whatever barriers keep the path to the Spirit cluttered and inaccessible. These barriers may be your insecurities, disbeliefs, misunderstandings or a history of painful encounters with others who professed to have a deep spiritual life. The most important part of awareness is the understanding that we, ourselves, have built elaborate barriers on the path to our Spirit. A spiritual guide may be able to help you identify those barriers, but only you can remove them.

Developing Inner Awareness

Inner awareness begins with a more deliberate and intentional adjustment toward the Spirit and toward yourself. When you are aware of your Spirit, life is more appropriately paced. Inner awareness allows life to be lived at a slower, conscious, more intentional level. In the stillness, you regain your equilibrium by becoming fully aware of your body, your mind and your Spirit.

If we practice using all of our senses on a daily basis, awareness becomes a natural part of life. We develop an ear for our Spirit. When the static in our lives is silenced, it is amazing how clearly we can hear the Spirit within speak to us.

Inner awareness allows us to know when we are having a spiritual experience and when we are receiving guidance from the Spirit. Cultivate the quiet, embrace the stillness and prepare to be amazed. Inner awareness, in and of itself, is not enough to fully develop your spiritual path, but it is a huge step forward.

Coloring Outside the Lines

Receptivity to the spiritual voice is expanded when you learn to let go of your expectations about what a "spiritual experience" should look like. Instead of putting your faith in the outcome, which puts a condition on the Spirit, you must put faith in the presence and flow of the Spirit and your interaction with that Spiritual force. Then you are free to experience your Spiritual self without judgment or reservation.

Letting Go of Expectation

Part of developing faith is having faith in yourself and your ability to listen to the Spirit. Faith is exercised in the giving away of something without an expectation or condition attached to the giving, but you must learn to give your gifts *only* to those who can appreciate them. When a gift is given unconditionally to one who appreciates the gift, you are fulfilled in the giving.

One of the hardest lessons I had to learn, and one I am still learning, is how to give love. We all want to *get* love, but the love we get is not the most fulfilling. It is the love we *give* that is most fulfilling. Giving love unconditionally is very rewarding if given to a person who appreciates the love they receive. When love is given to someone who cannot, or will not, appreciate the gift, we feel empty and our capacity to give love is diminished. When our love is given unconditionally to a person who recognizes and appreciates the gift, we are fulfilled and renewed in the love we have given.

Tuning in to the Spirit

Learning to be receptive to the Spirit is a key part of our Spiritual journey. When we take time to become aware and practice receptivity, we make the necessary adjustment in our lives to be in *tune* with the Spirit and thus spiritually fulfilled. When we are fulfilled, we receive exactly what we need from the Spirit and from life.

Practice and Patience: Ears of the Spirit

As you nurture the process of awareness, you will learn that patience is a foundational element.

I have learned if I allow things to happen naturally, things are still accomplished in a timely manner, but instead of being drained by the work, I am energized. Awareness, and a clear path to the Spirit, allows me to be guided and paced internally, rather than by some external control. In other words, I have greater control over my life when I allow the Spirit to lead.

Patience works. The interesting thing is that events occur whether I wait for them to happen or not. What I have learned is that by having patience, my human being will not get in the way of my Spirit being. When I allow the Spirit to guide my life, it flows smoother, more naturally, with less stress and strain. Ultimately, I am more fulfilled in my life and have more energy to enjoy life. Once we acknowledge and develop access to our Spirit, we broaden our ability to communicate with others on a less restrictive, deeper level. When we are spiritually aware, and spiritually fulfilled, we learn to communicate Spirit to Spirit with other people.

Passion: The Motor of Our Lives

Reaching out to others is not just to teach them about Spiritual things, but it is also teaching them about living a balanced life. Teaching others is about sharing our information, our skill and our Spirit. If what we do for our life's work connects us with our Spirit, then we are fueled by passion for the work. If we are fueled by passion, then we are constantly fulfilled and we are re-energized and renewed in our efforts to continue the work we enjoy.

There is nothing more fulfilling to me than the opportunity to emotionally touch people, to help them heal and grow, and then, to turn around and give away all the knowledge I have gained from my work so others learn to heal and help. I have nothing to lose by giving away all that I know.

The gift of my knowledge makes me a better person and allows the next person to continue the work I have started and expand on the knowledge I have shared. Each time I share my knowledge and wisdom my passion for my life's work grows.

Refueling Our Passion: Service

Understanding the Spirit is universal and also personal brings us to know that passionate service is what fuels our spiritual path. It is in the giving away of ourselves that we are renewed and replenished spiritually. When we have nurtured our Spirit by looking to what fulfills us, *and* by pursuing our passion, we will be more able to connect with the Light when we die. Although reassuring, reconnection with the Light cannot be the sum of our life goals. The goal of our Spiritual path must be in giving away what we have learned to others around us and perpetuating spiritual growth in the human dimension.

The secret to learning how to give is to start small and participate in the present moment of life. Giving can be as simple as giving a smile to someone who needs one. Passionate giving mandates that we are passionately living, paying attention to life and being aware of all that is going on around us.

Being aware of our environment provides us with multiple opportunities to practice this spiritual truth of giving. It is the single, consistent, individual, multiple passionate acts of giving, and being of service to others, which makes change in the lives of other people and impacts the human race on a global level.

What I have learned over the years about my experience in the Light, and with my own Spirit, is it has changed me and made me a better person than I would have otherwise been. The changes didn't happen overnight, but rather they happened over time.

So it is that the inspiration, passion, love and caring we give or receive from others is developed over time. It is important to realize we do not always get immediate confirmation when we give of ourselves, or give our skill and knowledge. The giving must be done with no expectation of any return.

The Magic of Faith and Passion

As we give away our knowledge, passion and Spirit, we begin to trust that the Spirit brings to us the person or persons who are most in need of what we have to offer. Additionally, as we become more in tune with our Spirit, we attract people into our lives who are also in tune with their spiritual-self and bring with them the spiritual lessons *we* need to learn, as well as the Spiritual energy that replenishes us.

Faith comes into play when we freely give away what we know without an agenda attached or without an investment in the outcome. How a particular individual implements what we share with them is not our concern. Our part is to have faith the Spirit will come alive in that person from what we have shared with them.

Faith is the anchor that allows us to freely share and give what we have without worry we will lose something or that we must control the outcome of our giving. Our gift is for the giving and the person who receives our gift is responsible for sorting out what is useful for their lives and what is not. When we allow another to use what we have given them without strings attached, we allow them to grow unfettered by expectation.

The greatest test of our faith is having the courage to believe in the wonderfulness and worthiness of ourselves. As we give our gifts, others are giving theirs. We must find a way to put ourselves in the midst of opportunities for growth and spiritual development so that we may accept those gifts that are made available to us.

If we are walking our spiritual path, the opportunities will be presented to us and we will be able to grasp them in a natural way. We must be ready to take advantage of those opportunities without hesitation.

Living life in a manner that grasps opportunities as they naturally come to us means we not only grasp the opportunity, but we also employ the opportunity when it arrives. We can use the opportunity to create what we want from life, and as we become more aware of our needs, we learn to sort through the opportunities and make use of only those that are most productive for us.

When you are on your spiritual path, you will become more aware. The Spirit will help you to become more aware. When you have accepted your Spirit, you can then more clearly see the opportunities as they are coming to you and recognize them as such. Spiritual awareness helps you to regain a proper spiritual posture.

Abundance: Teaching Others to Give It Away

When our desire to teach others is a result of being fulfilled in our Spirit, we are no longer fearful that someone will consume our knowledge or exploit us. When our knowledge is given away in this manner, there is an abundance of freedom that accompanies this type of benevolence. The knowledge given away is no longer a possession to wield power, gain position or influence in life, but rather it is a gift we share out of our abundance, and from the heart.

Giving away our knowledge is more than filling another person with intellectual information; it is about connecting with that person and passing along the energy and revitalization that is gained from being guided by the Spirit.

Giving away our Spirit to others has to do with passing along the spiritual energy that we have as well. Sometimes this is far more important than any verbiage we could give. When there is a spiritual connection, it is a far more powerful exchange than mere words. A spiritual connection ignites greater understanding, sensitivity and an emotional depth that is not possible with words. I believe teaching others by giving our Spiritual energy can move us one level closer to the dimension beyond this life.

Each and every time I freely give away my knowledge or wisdom from a sense of abundance and not fear, I receive twice in return what I have given. Yet the person who is on the receiving end claims that they are the one who has received more. There can be only one explanation: the spiritual energy multiplied upon itself. The type of spiritual energy that flows between us in our connection with one another multiplies itself in the exchange. The more knowledge we give away, the more fulfillment and energy we receive.

Fully Human, Fully Alive

When we are in touch with the Spirit, we are able to fully embrace our own humanity. To fully embrace our humanity means that we not only embrace the parts of ourselves that are strong and noble, but also embrace the parts of ourselves that are flawed, fallible and flailing about. Spiritual people are not necessarily perfect in their emotions or their deeds, but are able to accept their human imperfections by being aware of what needs to be done to improve themselves.

Sometimes, the lesson of fully embracing our humanity is one in which we learn to fully experience some part of our lives that is painful. Pain and sadness are as much a part of normal, natural life as happiness and contentment. The Spirit ultimately empowers us to live our lives to the fullest capacity, even when life inflicts pain upon us or when we suffer pain and sadness as a result of our own actions. When we live life to the fullest extent, we are fulfilled, regardless.

Fulfillment comes in the recognition that pain is a normal part of living. We learn emotional pain is part of being an emotional being and physical pain is part of being a physical being. What we fail to realize most often is we can be completely fulfilled in our lives, even when we are at a painful juncture.

The Road to Fulfillment

When we are fulfilled, we are productive, the kind of productivity that gives meaning to our lives. Fulfillment does not come easy. It's not just handed to us. The goal is to be fulfilled in all that we do, not just when things are going our way. It means being *full* of our Spirit at all times, in all places. It means trusting the Spirit will not lead us astray. It means taking action and trusting the Spirit will bring us the resources that we need. It is about having the faith that each new day will bring new opportunities and that each new opportunity will bring new experiences and healing.

If there is only one lesson that you take from this book, or from my story, it is to always hold yourself in high esteem, to believe deeply in yourself. Because **YOU** are the Spirit. **YOU** are the source of your own fulfillment.

When you are content with yourself, you will be fulfilled. Fulfillment is built on self-acceptance and self-acceptance is gained through your Spiritual awareness. To be truly fulfilled, we must each seek our own path.

When you pay attention to yourself and practice good self-care, both emotionally and spiritually, your life becomes more dynamic. You will attract opportunities and people in your life that you never dreamed possible. Your source of energy, the Spirit, multiplies within you and fills you completely.

The more fulfilled you become by the Spirit, the more you will realize you have an entire lifetime ahead of you, regardless of age. Finding fulfillment is not the end of the road, it is just the beginning. It's a time when life is booming, and growing, and full of opportunities, special events and special people. Please, if you do nothing else in your life, find your Spirit. Find your source of fulfillment. Fulfillment is what gives value to life.

Letting Go of Control

When we stop insisting on controlling every aspect of our lives and simply allow life to happen, be it painful or happy, we can stop trying to control the Spirit. The Spirit then intervenes unconsciously and moves us cleanly through a situation without a great deal of complication.

There is nothing mysterious about following the Spirit and abandoning our fears, worries and concerns. The process of gaining awareness is to be still, wait and reflect. It is quite possible to learn the process of stillness, patience and reflection in the daily activity of everyday life by letting go of fear and control.

The fear of death is one of the most controlling factors in our lives, but to the enlightened mind, death is only the beginning of the next great adventure. Letting go of the fear of death allows life to be lived fully, to its natural conclusion.

The End

Life is never-ending; the Spirit lives on for eternity. One of my higher purposes for being in this dimension at this time is to share with you what I know about the Spirit. This knowledge is based on my moment in the Light and my experiences in life. Someday, I will again leave this human life and resume a life in the Spiritual dimension.

Until that time I will continue to share all I know about Spirituality and human life. It is not my desire to convince you there is a Spirit, or a Spiritual dimension. I am only here to share what I know in my heart. That is my unconditional gift. What you do with that gift is entirely up to you.

If morning never comes... are *you* ready for the next dimension?

BILL VANDENBUSH

FROM THE AUTHOR

"A tragedy of war nearly destroyed my life, but a spiritual force intervened and has guided me on an incredible lifelong journey. Come join me on this journey and learn how the Spirit taught me to overcome overwhelming odds and find my purpose in life. Let me share with you the insights and lessons I learned from an excursion into a dimension of enlightenment."

Bill VandenBush served in Vietnam from July 1968 to April 1969. He was with C Company 3/1 11th LIB Americal Division. Currently retired, he lives in Washington State where he continues to write and promote his ideals.

To order an autographed copy of Bill's book, send $14.95 plus $4.00 shipping and handling to:

Bill VandenBush
P O Box 65286
University Place, WA 98464-1286
(or use the order blank on the last page of this book)

Bill is an inspiring speaker. He has appeared on Arthur C. Clark's *Mysterious Universe, Sightings, Town Meetings* and several near-death experience PBS specials. He has frequently shared his story at the International Association for Near Death Studies and with numerous community organizations, colleges, high schools and church groups. Contact him at the address above (or through The Old Hundred and One Press) to invite him speak at your meeting, event or workshop.

From THE OLD 101 PRESS:

"They say you can't take it with you,
but you can.
When you die,
all the stories in your head go, too."

Billie Thornburg, founder of the Old Hundred and One Press and author of *Bertie and Me* and *Bertie and Me and Miles Too* is dedicated to encouraging people to write the stories of their lives. At age ninety she started The Old Hundred and One Press to publish history as told by those who've lived it.

Write your memories and send them to:

The Old Hundred and One Press
13680 Sandhill Road
North Platte, NE 69101

www.theold101press.com
Phone: 308-534-0144
Fax: 308-534-0145

If you havewritten a book to be published, query with the first 20 pages. Manuscripts should be double-spaced. Include a SASE and please allow six weeks for a response.

We're also assembling a book of stories about life in the Midwest called *City and Prairie Bones*. To be included, send your complete manuscript to the above address.

Available From The Old Hundred and One Press:

If Morning Never Comes　by Bill Vandebush. The powerful story of a soldier's near death experience in Vietnam. "A priceless gift to anyone in search of their own spiritual path...enormously inspirational."

From a review by Nora Fitzgerald

Bertie and Me　, Billie Snyder Thornburg's first book. A humorous and historical account of two little girls growing up on a Nebraska Sandhill ranch in the early 1900s.

Bertie and Me and Miles　Too　, Billie Snyder Thornburg continues telling of early Sandhill life with stories about her brother Miles, home remedies, Model T's, privies and old time roundups.

Coming in October 2003:

Ask Me If I'm A Worm by Ann Milton. The second in a science series that teaches children about nature by comparing a kid's body to that of a worm. The first of the Ask Me Series, *Ask Me If I'm A Frog*, won the John Burroughs Nature Book Award.

ORDER FORM

If Morning Never Comes By Bill VandenBush
Bertie and Me By Billie Thornburg
Bertie and Me and Miles Too By Billie Thornburg
Ask Me If I'm A Frog By Ann Milton
Ask Me If I'm A Worm By Ann Milton

Order by
Fax :   308-534-0145
Phone: 308-534-0144
Website: www.theold101press.com
Email: annmilton@inebraska.com
Post::   The Old Hundred and One Press
            13680 N Sandhill Road
            North Platte, NE 69101

Send ____ copies of *If Morning Never Comes* @ $14.95
Send ____ copies of *Bertie and Me* @ $18.95
Send ____ copies of *Bertie and Me and Miles Too* @ $16.95
Send ____ copies of *Ask Me If I'm A Frog* @ $8.95
Send ____ copies of *Ask Me If I'm A Worm* @ $8.95

Please add $4.00 for shipping and handling

TOTAL ENCLOSED: _____

Name:_____
Address:_____
City, State, ZIP:

These books may also be purchased in bookstores, on
www.amazon.com or from Baker and Taylor.